DEVELOPMEN

IN PRACTIC

Higher
Education

Higher
Education

The Lessons
of Experience

THE WORLD BANK
WASHINGTON, D. C.

The Development in Practice series publishes reviews of the World
Bank's activities in different regions and sectors. It lays particular
emphasis on the progress that is being made and on the policies and
practices that hold the most promise of success in the effort to reduce
poverty in the developing world.

This book is a product of the staff of the World Bank, and the
judgments made herein do not necessarily reflect the view of its Board
of Directors or the governments they represent.

The photograph on the cover shows a trainee technician in Dakar, Senegal.
Courtesy Curt Carnemark.

Library of Congress Cataloging-in-Publication Data

Higher education: the lessons of experience.
      p.   cm. — (Development in practice)
   Includes bibliographical references (p.   ).
   ISBN 0-8213-2745-3
   1. Education, Higher—Finance—Case studies. 2. Education,
Higher—Economic aspects—Case studies. 3. Educational change—Case
studies. I. International Bank for Reconstruction and Development.
II. Series: Development in practice (Washington, D.C.)
LB2341.H525   1994
378'.02—dc20   94-8891
                                             CIP

Contents

Foreword

UNIVERSITIES educate future leaders and develop the high-level technical capacities that underpin economic growth. Developing countries have invested heavily in their universities and other institutions of higher learning. During the past twenty years, enrollments have increased on average by 6.2 percent per year in low- and lower-middle-income countries, and by 7.3 percent per year in upper-middle-income countries. Sources of external finance such as the World Bank have helped to underwrite this expansion.

Rapid enrollment growth in many countries may have contributed, however, to a deterioration in quality. Pressures on public resources have led to the neglect of key inputs to instruction and research. Furthermore, public subsidies as a proportion of unit costs of higher education often far exceed the subsidies to primary and secondary education. Because students in higher education tend to come from the higher-income groups, a large publicly funded higher education system tends to have adverse effects on income distribution. The need to implement comprehensive reform is widely acknowledged.

This study draws on the World Bank's operational and policy analysis experience, a review of existing literature, and original studies. Broad consultation was undertaken with higher education policymakers in developing countries, representatives of external finance agencies, and acknowledged experts from the academic world. The objective of this study is to draw lessons from recent experience to inform and sharpen policy discussion both in the Bank and among our borrowers.

The study is part of a broader search for ways to improve the effectiveness of World Bank support for education. The work program began with two Policy Papers, *Primary Education* (World Bank 1990) and *Vocational and Technical Education and Training* (World Bank 1991b). This report on higher education is the third in the series. An overview paper on education policy is now being produced that will summarize the issues and policy recommendations for the education sector as a whole.

This report examines the main dimensions of the higher education crisis in developing countries and assesses the prospects for successful reform. In exploring strategies and options to improve the performance of higher education systems, it focuses on four main directions for reform: greater differentiation of higher education institutions, including the development of private institutions; diversification of funding sources for public higher education; a redefinition of the role of the state in higher education, with greater emphasis on institutional autonomy and accountability; and an emphasis on the importance of policies explicitly designed to give priority to quality and equity objectives.

Bringing about change is a difficult task, but significant reforms have already taken place in many countries. The report draws lessons from international experiences in reform, and it provides a menu of policy options for countries looking for ways to improve the contribution of higher education to economic and social development.

Armeane M. Choksi
Vice President
Human Resources Development and Operations Policy
The World Bank

Preface

THE PURPOSE of this study is to highlight and make widely available the lessons of experience with higher education in many countries. It brings together the results of a large number of thematic reports and regional case studies on higher education either specifically commissioned for the study or prepared as part of the regular activities of World Bank operational departments.

Much emphasis was put on external consultation in preparing the study. The work program was guided by a series of international and regional meetings that brought together leaders in higher education from industrial and developing countries, representatives of lending and aid agencies, and members of higher education associations. This consultative process proved a valuable channel for sharing information and receiving constructive feedback to guide the study. The study was discussed by the Executive Directors of the World Bank on October 15, 1993.

In view of the growing complexity and diversity of modern higher education systems, this study uses a generic definition of higher education that encompasses all formal post-secondary institutions that train middle- and high-level professional personnel in degree-, diploma-, and certificate-granting programs. The terms higher education, tertiary education, and post-secondary education are used interchangeably in this document.

While the focus of this study is on the developing countries of Africa, Asia, and Latin America, the specific circumstances of the former socialist republics of Europe and Central Asia, which are in a process of rapid economic transition, are also discussed where appropriate.

This study was prepared by a team led by Jamil Salmi and comprising Douglas Albrecht, Robin DePietro-Jurand, Tom Eisemon, Moussa Kourouma,

Omporn Regel, Viswanathan Selvaratnam, Erik Thulstrup, Kin Bing Wu, and Adrian Ziderman. The background papers and the initial draft of the study were prepared under the general direction of Ann O. Hamilton and the immediate supervision of Adriaan M. Verspoor in the World Bank's Population and Human Resources Department. The study was completed under the general direction of K. Y. Amoako and the immediate supervision of Peter R. Moock in the Bank's Education and Social Policy Department. Margareta J. Verbeeck prepared it for publication.

Executive Summary

The Challenges and the Constraints

Higher education is of paramount importance for economic and social development. Institutions of higher education have the main responsibility for equipping individuals with the advanced knowledge and skills required for positions of responsibility in government, business, and the professions. These institutions produce new knowledge through research, serve as conduits for the transfer, adaptation, and dissemination of knowledge generated elsewhere in the world, and support government and business with advice and consultancy services. In most countries, higher education institutions also play important social roles by forging the national identity of the country and offering a forum for pluralistic debate. The development of higher education is correlated with economic development: enrollment ratios in higher education average 51 percent in the countries that belong to the Organization for Economic Cooperation and Development (OECD), compared with 21 percent in middle-income countries and 6 percent in low-income countries. Estimated social rates of return of 10 percent or more in many developing countries also indicate that investments in higher education contribute to increases in labor productivity and to higher long-term economic growth, which are essential for poverty alleviation.

Higher Education in Crisis

Despite the clear importance of investment in higher education for economic growth and social development, the sector is in crisis throughout the world. In all countries, higher education is heavily dependent on government funding. In an era of widespread fiscal constraints, industrial as well as developing countries are grappling with the challenge of preserving or improving the quality of higher education as education budgets—and particularly expenditures per student—are compressed.

The crisis is most acute in the developing world, both because fiscal adjustments have been harsher and because it has been more difficult for developing countries to contain pressures for enrollment expansion, given relatively low enrollment ratios. The result has been a dramatic compression of per student expenditures since the late 1970s—for example, in Sub-Saharan Africa from an average of $6,300 in 1980 to $1,500 in 1988. (Throughout the book, dollars are U.S. dollars unless specified.) To the extent that it results from a more efficient use of resources, lower spending per student is desirable, but the quality of teaching and research has deteriorated precipitously in many countries. In these countries, higher education institutions operate under adverse conditions: overcrowding, deteriorating physical facilities, and lack of resources for nonsalary expenditures such as textbooks, educational materials, laboratory consumables, and maintenance. Reflecting the sluggish growth of aggregate demand for highly skilled labor, graduate unemployment in developing countries rose sharply during the 1980s and continues to rise.

In most developing countries, higher education has been the fastest-growing segment of the education system during the past twenty years, with enrollments increasing on average by 6.2 percent per year in low- and lower-middle-income countries and 7.3 percent per year in upper-middle-income countries. This rapid increase has been driven by high levels of subsidization and, in some cases, guaranteed government employment of graduates. In most cases, the outcome of these policies has been fiscally unsustainable enrollment growth and a sharp decline in quality. The decline in academic standards in primary and secondary education has also affected the performance of higher education systems. While the rapid growth of enrollments has led to increased access to higher education for traditionally less privileged populations, including women and students of rural origin, higher education generally remains elitist, with the majority of students coming from wealthier families.

Despite the fact that female enrollment rates have grown faster than male enrollment rates, women are still sorely underrepresented in higher education in many countries. While male and female enrollment ratios are relatively equal in the former socialist countries of Eastern and Central Europe and in some Latin American countries (for example, Brazil), in 1989 women accounted for only 25 percent of enrollments in Africa, 35 percent in Asia, 36 percent in the Middle East and North Africa, and 47 percent in Latin America and the Caribbean.

Compounding the problem of declining resources per student is the inefficient use of these resources. Higher education in many developing countries is characterized by low student-staff ratios, underutilized facilities, duplicative program offerings, high dropout and repetition rates, and a very large share of the budget devoted to noneducational expenditures, such as subsidized student housing, food, and other services. In one Latin American country, for instance, costs per graduate in public universities are seven times higher than in private universities because of the higher repetition and dropout rates. In many francophone African countries, more than 50 percent of the total higher education budget is spent on noneducational student subsidies. These high subsidies to public university students are not only an inefficient educational investment but also regressive social spending, because students enrolled in universities are disproportionately from the upper end of the income distribution.

A number of OECD countries have responded to the funding crisis by introducing innovative policies during the past decade aimed at increasing the efficiency of higher education (such as the Netherlands' use of funding formulas) and stimulating greater private funding (as in Australia and Ireland). Despite the relentless fiscal pressures that most developing countries face, few have made significant progress in the area of higher education reform. Yet the experience of a few developing countries such as Chile indicates that it is possible to achieve a well-functioning, diversified, and growing higher education system even as public spending per student declines.

Indeed, it is arguable that higher education should not have the highest-priority claim on incremental public resources available for education in many developing countries, especially those that have not yet achieved adequate access, equity, and quality at the primary and secondary levels. This is because of the priority that countries attach to achieving universal literacy; because the social rates of return on investments in primary and secondary education usually exceed the returns on higher education; and because investments in basic education can also improve equity because they tend to reduce income inequalities. Each country needs to weigh carefully the right balance of resource allocation between the three education subsectors, considering the relative social rates of return at each level as well as the complementarity which exists between primary, secondary, and tertiary education. Furthermore, the overwhelming fiscal reality in most developing countries is such that quality improvements and enrollment expansion in higher education will have to be achieved with little or no increase in public expenditures.

Strategies for Reform

This report analyzes the lessons of experience to show how developing countries can achieve the goals of greater efficiency, quality, and equity in higher education. It documents the depth of the crisis affecting higher education systems throughout the developing world, notwithstanding variations in the size, diversity, public/private split, and funding levels which characterize the sector in different countries. A review of country experience suggests four key directions for reform:

- Encouraging greater differentiation of institutions, including the development of private institutions
- Providing incentives for public institutions to diversify sources of funding, including cost-sharing with students, and linking government funding closely to performance
- Redefining the role of government in higher education
- Introducing policies explicitly designed to give priority to quality and equity objectives.

Reform requirements and political and economic conditions vary considerably across regions, and there is no single blueprint appropriate for every country. While the four key directions given above constitute broad areas for reform, the pace of implementing reforms and the relative importance of various options will obviously depend on specific country circumstances such as the level of income and the degree of education development (for example, primary and secondary level coverage, and the existence of private institutions). This book draws lessons from a wide range of country experiences in order to inform the process of policy analysis and policy choice in developing countries intent upon improving the equity, efficiency, and quality of their higher education systems.

In no country will achieving these reforms be easy. The predominant pattern of public higher education in the developing world principally benefits the most affluent households, who are also the most powerful politically. The children of the well-off are heavily subsidized by the rest of society to attend public universities, reinforcing their economic and social advantage. Experience demonstrates that breaking this pattern is essential, and also that the political difficulty of doing so should not be underestimated. In countries with fragile systems of governance, students with grievances—and there will be grievances if subsidies and privileges are reduced—can represent a threat to political stability. Governments therefore necessarily tread warily in introducing reforms that affect the most powerful households and those with the potential to destabilize political regimes.

Differentiating Institutions and Expanding Private Provision

The traditional model of the European research university, with its one-tier program structure, has proven expensive and inappropriate in the developing world. Increased differentiation in higher education, or the development of non-university institutions and encouragement of private institutions, can help meet the growing social demand for higher education and make higher education systems more responsive to changing labor market needs. Asia is the continent where differentiation efforts have been the most extensive and the most effective and which has the most lessons for the rest of the developing world. Governments in Asia spend less per student on higher education than in other regions, but achieve higher coverage because they have been able to lower average costs and mobilize private funding through increased differentiation.

Developing Non-University Institutions

In recent years, non-university higher education institutions, both public and private, have grown faster than universities. Non-university institutions include polytechnics, short-cycle professional and technical institutes, community colleges, and distance education and open learning programs. Their lower-cost programs make them both attractive to students and easier for private providers to set up. In the most successful cases, non-university institutions offer training that responds flexibly to labor market demands and is linked with university programs through appropriate transfer mechanisms such as credit systems and equivalency provisions.

Encouraging Private Provision of Higher Education

Private institutions are an important element of some of the strongest higher education systems to be found today in developing countries. They can respond efficiently and flexibly to changing demand, and they increase educational opportunities with little or no additional public cost. Governments can encourage the development of private higher education to complement public institutions as a means of managing the costs of expanding higher education enrollments, increasing the diversity of training programs, and broadening social participation in higher education.

A key finding from successful examples is that government encouragement of a sound private sector in higher education requires a policy and regulatory framework which avoids disincentives such as tuition price controls, and includes mechanisms for accreditation, oversight, and evaluation of private institutions. Some countries have also provided financial incentives to stimulate the development of private institutions on the grounds that these provide a means of expanding enrollments at lower public cost. Making public funding for quality improvements available to both private and public institutions on the basis of the quality of their proposals serves the long-term objective of establishing a level playing field for all higher education institutions, public and private alike. Competition for public resources has been used as a stimulus for improved quality and increased efficiency in Chile, and on a more limited scale in Brazil and the Republic of Korea with competitive processes for research funding.

Diversifying the Funding of Public Institutions and Introducing Incentives for Their Performance

Public institutions will continue to educate a large share, if not the majority, of students in most countries, even if the role of the private sector is strengthened and most *new* enrollments are channeled to private institutions. Experience shows that if public institutions are to achieve higher quality and greater efficiency, governments will need to implement sweeping reforms in financing designed to: (1) encourage the mobilization of greater private financing of higher education, (2) provide support to qualified students unable to pursue their studies for reasons of inadequate family income, and (3) foster efficiency in allocating and using public resources among and within institutions.

Mobilizing Greater Private Financing

Cost-sharing with students. The financial base of public higher education can be strengthened by mobilizing a greater share of the necessary financing from students themselves, who can expect significantly greater lifetime earnings as a result of receiving higher education and who often come from families with ample ability to contribute to the costs of their education. Cost-sharing can be pursued through tuition fees and the elimination of subsidies for noninstructional costs. Governments can permit public institutions to establish their own tuition and fees without interference, although governments have an important role to play in making objective information about school quality available to prospective students. Countries can also reduce sharply, if not eliminate, the subsidization of noninstructional expenditures such as housing and meals. In Botswana and Ghana, for instance, subsidies for student meals have been eliminated, the catering function has been privatized, and significant cost savings have been achieved.

Funding from alumni and external aid and lending agencies. A second source of private resources is donations and endowments from alumni and private industry. In some countries, notably the United States and United Kingdom, alumni contributions represent a significant source of discretionary income for higher education institutions. This kind of philanthropy can be encouraged by favorable tax regimes. The establishment of trust funds with initial support from external aid and lending agencies also can be a useful form of endowment, especially in small states with a limited economic base.

Income-generating activities. Governments can encourage public higher education institutions to pursue income-generating activities such as short-term courses, contract research for industry, and consultancy services. The first step is to eliminate the *disincentive* many countries create by reducing government budget allocations to public institutions to offset any incremental resources they raise from outside sources. Governments can create positive incentives by matching the funds raised from outside income.

In sum, increased private financial support for higher education mobilized through the elimination of noninstructional subsidies, the introduction of fees, the pursuit of donations, and the undertaking of income-generating activities can provide institutions with a more diversified and likely more stable funding base. An indicative target could be for public institutions to generate income covering 30 percent of recurrent expenditures from these nongovernment sources. Several countries have already achieved this percentage with tuition fees alone. The time required to reach this target will vary with country circumstances, however, and countries such as Chile, Jordan, and Korea that have already achieved this degree of active mobilization of funds from the private sector may well want to go further. In addition to reducing their dependence on public financing and their vulnerability to budget fluctuations, cost-sharing makes public institutions more responsive to market signals. Cost-sharing with students also creates important incentives for students to select their programs of study carefully and to complete their studies more rapidly.

A critical feature of any policy to encourage the diversification of higher education funding is to allow incremental resources to remain available in significant measure for use in the institutions that mobilize them. Policies that seek to expropriate resources obtained by the efforts of individual institutions for use by a central authority are self-defeating because they destroy the institutions' incentive to look for savings or generate income.

Financial Support to Needy Students

Cost-sharing cannot be implemented equitably without a functioning student loan program to assist students who need to borrow for their education and without scholarship programs that guarantee necessary financial support to academically qualified poor students unable to absorb the direct and indirect (forgone earnings) costs of higher education.

Governments can improve the efficiency of existing student loan schemes and broaden their coverage. Experience to date with existing loan schemes in about fifty industrial and developing countries has been disappointing. Because of heavily subsidized interest rates, high default rates, and high administrative costs, the financial performance of loan schemes has been unsatisfactory. But the experiences of Colombia and the Canadian province of Quebec, for example, show that it is possible to design and administer financially sustainable programs.

Income-contingent loan schemes, being adopted by a growing number of countries, can be more efficient and equitable than traditional loan schemes, if national income tax and social security authorities have the administrative capacity to handle loan collection efficiently.

Equity can also be enhanced by grant schemes targeted to the lowest-income students and by work-study programs. Financial assistance programs that are administered by a central agency (such as in the United Kingdom and United States), and that allow students to take their assistance package to any institution of their choosing, have an important advantage over programs administered by individual institutions. Such "student-based" or "portable" assistance enables poor students to make the same choices as those with more financial resources and stimulates competition among educational institutions to offer programs in line with student demand. In this way, governments can use market forces to stimulate increases in the quality and efficiency of higher education.

Incentives for Efficient Resource Allocation and Utilization

The distribution of public resources to tertiary institutions in most countries is based on negotiated budgets. This fails to provide incentives for efficient operation and quality improvement and makes it difficult to adjust the distribution of financial resources to changing circumstances. Alternative mechanisms that link funding to performance criteria are being used increasingly by OECD countries and could be considered by developing countries as well. Chile's innovative program to channel funding to public and private institutions on the basis of the number of top-quality students they attract stimulates institutions to improve their quality. Such funding mechanisms create powerful incentives for higher quality and/or more efficient use of resources.

Redefining the Role of Government

The types of reforms discussed above imply profound changes in the relationship between government and the higher education establishment in many countries. For most countries, they also imply considerable expansion of the private sector in higher education. Nonetheless, there are clear economic justifications for continued state support of higher education:

■ Higher education investments generate external benefits important for economic development, such as the long-term returns on basic research and on technology development and transfer; because these benefits cannot be captured by individuals, they result in socially suboptimal private investment in higher education

■ Imperfections in capital markets curtail the ability of individuals to borrow adequately for education, which reduces, in particular, the participation of meritorious but economically disadvantaged groups in higher education.

In most developing countries, however, the extent of government involvement in higher education has far exceeded what is economically efficient. The crisis of higher education, particularly in the public sector, is stimulating a change in the extent, objectives, and modalities of government intervention in higher education in order to ensure a more efficient use of public resources. Rather than direct control, the government's responsibility is becoming that of providing an enabling policy environment for both public and private higher education institutions and of using the leverage of public funding to stimulate these institutions to meet national training and research needs efficiently. Successful implementation of higher education reforms has been shown to depend on: (1) the establishment of a coherent policy framework; (2) greater reliance on incentives and market-oriented instruments to implement policies; and (3) increased management autonomy for public institutions.

A Coherent Policy Framework

More differentiated higher education systems require a well-defined legal framework and consistent policies. They require a vision on the part of policymakers for the sector as a whole and for the role of each type of institution within that whole, including private institutions. Small but capable independent oversight agencies can formulate and monitor higher education policies, guide budgetary allocations, and evaluate and publicize institutions' performance for the benefit of prospective students.

Greater Reliance on Incentive Instruments to Implement Policies

Where circumstances require correction of labor market and enrollment distortions, governments do best to rely on student incentives such as scholarships and student loans and on resource allocation processes rather than issuing directives to institutions regarding their student intake. For students to make rational choices, however, they need good information on the costs and quality of courses at different institutions and on the labor market opportunities for graduates of different courses. Governments can help strengthen the quality of education by ensuring that such information is widely available (for example, on institutions' costs, relative performance, and on salaries in the labor market) and by certifying quality through accreditation. Governments can either accredit higher education institutions themselves, although this can be very demanding on resources, or allow private accrediting agencies and professional associations to perform this function.

Increased Autonomy for Public Institutions

Decentralization of all key management functions (including the power to set fees, recruit and retrench personnel, and use budgetary allocations flexibly across expenditure categories) to higher education institutions themselves is a sine qua non for successful reform, especially with respect to funding diversification and more efficient use of resources. Institutions cannot respond to incentives to improve quality and efficiency without control over their resources and processes. Along with increased autonomy, however, higher education institutions need to be held accountable for their academic and management performance. This requires more sophisticated evaluation criteria and oversight capacity than most governments have in place today.

Focusing on Quality, Responsiveness, and Equity

Priority objectives for higher education reform, against which progress can be measured, are: (1) increased quality of teaching and research; (2) increased responsiveness of higher education to labor market demands; and (3) increased equity.

Enhancing the Quality of Training and Research

High-quality training and research require well-prepared students. This preparation, in turn, is determined by the quality of academic primary and secondary education and the selection process for higher education. A high-quality and well-motivated teaching staff and a supportive professional culture are essential. Universities also need sufficient pedagogical inputs including cost-effective access to up-to-date information through electronic networks and CD-ROM. Finally, an important determinant of academic performance is the ability to evaluate and monitor the quality of training and research outputs. The most effective evaluation mechanisms emphasize self-evaluation of an institution's mission and performance combined with external assessment, whether by professional associations or a government oversight agency.

Because they have limited human and financial resources, difficulty in taking advantage of economies of scale, and a modest-size labor market, small and low-income countries face specific constraints on the size of higher education systems that they can afford. These countries need to find an appropriate balance between institutions they can support locally, regional institutions, and overseas training. In many cases, the only cost-effective way of establishing or maintaining graduate training and research programs is to organize them on a regional basis. Each participating country would support a few strong national programs operating as regional centers of specialization within the framework of a multi-state institution such as the University of the South Pacific or the University of the West Indies.

Responding to Changing Economic Demands

In the context of economic growth strategies based on technological innovation, it is critically important that the institutions responsible for advanced training and research programs be guided by representatives from the productive sectors. The participation of private sector representatives on the governing boards of public and private higher education institutions can help ensure the relevance of academic programs. Financial incentives for joint industry-university cooperative research, corporate-sponsored internships for students, and part-time academic appointments for professionals from the productive sectors can all help strengthen the linkages and communication between the higher education system and other sectors of the economy. In the newly industrialized economies of East Asia, for instance, government-provided funding for cooperative research was a strong incentive for firms and universities to establish linkages. Continuing education programs are also an effective channel to respond to changing training requirements.

Pursuing Equity

Achieving greater equity of participation in higher education is important for economic efficiency, as well as for social justice and stability. Preferential admissions policies to increase the proportion of low-income ethnic minority and female students will not adversely affect higher education quality if overall selectivity is high, if remedial assistance is available, and if concomitant efforts are made to increase the average quality of secondary education. Ultimately, equity cannot be achieved in higher education unless women, low-income youths, and other disadvantaged subgroups of the population have access to good-quality public education at the preschool, primary, and secondary levels.

Implications for the World Bank

World Bank lending for higher education has a mixed record. In several countries, especially in the early years of lending for education, the Bank supported investments based on a narrow manpower rationale. Projects were mainly directed toward individual institutions and did not focus sufficiently on sectoral policy issues. As a result, some Bank-financed investments have proven to be unsustainable. The Bank has been most successful where it helped shape a coherent sub-sectoral development program and supported the implementation of policy reforms and investments through a series of lending operations, as in China. The three decades of World Bank education lending to Korea offer another example of a successful approach, which involved well-integrated support for investments to develop the national scientific training and research infrastructure as well as industrial capacity.

Higher education investments are important for economic growth. They increase individuals' productivity and incomes, as indicated by rate-of-return analysis, and they also produce significant external benefits not captured by such analysis, such as the long-term returns to basic research and to technology development and transfer. Economic growth is a critical prerequisite for sustained poverty reduction in developing countries, which is the overarching objective of the World Bank.

Within the education sector, however, there is evidence that higher education investments have lower social rates of return than investments in primary and secondary education and that investments in basic education can also have more direct impact on poverty reduction, because they tend to improve income equality. Recognizing this, developing countries throughout the world are investing heavily at these levels, and in primary education in particular; gross primary enrollment ratios increased from 79 to 104 percent between 1970 and 1990. This progress has been supported with World Bank lending, and primary and secondary education will continue to be the highest priority subsectors in the Bank's education lending to countries that have not yet achieved universal literacy and adequate access, equity, and quality at the primary and secondary levels. In these countries, our involvement in higher education will continue to be mainly to make its financing more equitable and cost-effective, so that primary and secondary education can receive increased attention at the margin.

Reform of higher education, and particularly strategies for mobilizing greater private financing for higher education through cost-sharing and the promotion of private institutions, can help countries free up some of the incremental public resources needed to improve quality and access at the primary and secondary levels. World Bank lending for higher education thus has a further strong justification: to support countries' efforts to adopt policy reforms that will allow the subsector to operate more efficiently and at lower public cost. Countries prepared to adopt a higher education policy framework that stresses a differentiated institutional structure and diversified resource base, with greater emphasis on private providers and private funding, will continue to receive priority. In these countries, Bank lending for higher education is supporting sector policy reforms, institutional development, and quality improvement.

Sector Policy Reforms

Reforms of the financing and management of higher education are necessary in many countries to establish a more equitable, efficient, and higher-quality system. Bank support for higher education generally takes place in an agreed-upon policy framework with monitorable benchmarks. While the composition of the package of policy reforms will vary by region and income level, reflecting each country's specific socioeconomic and political circumstances, in most cases it includes some combination of measures to: (1) control access to public higher education on the basis of efficient and equitable selection criteria; (2) encourage the development of institutions with different programs and different missions; (3) establish a positive environment for private institutions; (4) introduce or increase cost sharing and other financial diversification measures; (5) provide loan, grant, and work-study schemes to ensure that all qualified students have the opportunity to pursue higher education; (6) allocate public resources to higher education institutions in ways that are transparent and that strengthen quality and increase efficiency; and (7) provide autonomy in how public institutions raise and use resources and determine student intake.

Institutional Development

Support for institutional development will continue to aim at strengthening government policymaking and reform implementation as well as the planning and financial management of higher education institutions. At the national level, this implies: (1) establishing or strengthening oversight bodies with a capacity to analyze policy, evaluate funding requests, monitor institutions' performance, and make information about institutions' performance available to students; (2) introducing transparent mechanisms for the allocation of public higher education budgets; and (3) assisting countries to set up or restructure their student loan and financial assistance systems. At the institutional level, it consists of technical assistance and financial incentives to strengthen the managerial capacity of universities and other institutions and their ability to improve efficiency.

Quality Improvement

World Bank investments in higher education will continue to be integrated into national strategies that give explicit priority to improving the quality of instruction and research. This means that (1) Bank investments in higher education are increasingly targeted to support national and regional programs of excellence, whether public or private, (2) access to funding is more and more on a competitive basis, and (3) the Bank is supporting the establishment of accreditation and performance assessment systems.

CHAPTER ONE

The Challenges and the Constraints

HIGHER education contributes to human resource development in many ways. Investment in higher education can be a key contributor to a country's economic growth. Higher education institutions have the main responsibility for training a country's professional personnel, including the managers, scientists, engineers, and technicians who participate in the development, adaptation, and diffusion of innovations in the economy. Such institutions should create new knowledge through research and advanced training and serve as a conduit for its transfer, adaptation, and dissemination.

In most countries, higher education also plays important social roles by forging the national identity of the country and offering a forum for pluralistic debate. The development of higher education is correlated with economic development: enrollment ratios in higher education average 51 percent in the OECD countries, compared with 21 percent in middle-income countries and 6 percent in low-income countries.

During the past three decades, developing nations have invested considerable resources in their higher education systems, often with the support of external aid and lending agencies. Quantitatively, the results in many cases have surpassed expectations. In most countries, higher education has been the fastest-growing segment of the education system. Between 1965 and 1990, enrollment ratios increased very rapidly in most parts of the developing world: from 1 to 9 percent in North Africa, from 8 to 16 percent in the Middle East, from 7 to 21 percent in Latin America, and from 8 to 17 percent in East Asia. As a result of their investment in higher education, several developing countries have established a comprehensive infrastructure for advanced training, have fully indigenized their public bureaucracies, and have used their universities to foster national unity.

Higher Education in Crisis

Despite the clear importance of higher education for economic growth and social development, investment in the sector is in crisis in industrial as well as developing countries throughout the world. In all countries, higher education is heavily dependent on government funding, and unit costs are high relative to other segments of the education system. In an era of widespread fiscal constraints, industrial as well as developing countries are grappling with the challenge of how to preserve or improve the quality of higher education as education budgets—and particularly expenditures per student—are compressed.

The crisis is most acute in the developing world, both because fiscal adjustments have been harsher and because it has been more difficult for these countries to contain pressures for enrollment expansion, given relatively low enrollment ratios. In most developing countries, higher education has been the fastest-growing segment of the education system during the past twenty years, with enrollments increasing on average 6.2 percent per year in low- and lower-middle-income countries and 7.3 percent per year in upper-middle-income countries. This rapid increase has been driven by a high level of subsidization and in such cases, guaranteed government employment of graduates. While there are exceptions, the quality of teaching and research has declined sharply in public higher education institutions in the developing world. Many public systems operate with overcrowded and deteriorating physical facilities, inadequate staffing, poor library resources, and insufficient scientific equipment and instructional materials. Even in the former socialist nations of Europe and Central Asia, where the growth of enrollments was limited until 1989, drastic reductions in public funding are jeopardizing the quality and sustainability of existing programs and even the survival of institutions. In many countries, internal efficiency is very low and graduate unemployment continues to rise. Serious inequities in access and resource allocation (especially by socioeconomic origin and gender) also persist in many settings.

Resource Constraints

The number of students enrolled in higher education institutions continued to rise rapidly in the 1980s, reflecting the pressure of growing enrollments at the secondary level and intensified demand for higher education. Adverse macroeconomic conditions and increased competition for scarce public funds have reduced many governments' capacity to support higher education, and public expenditures for higher education have fallen. The two trends taken together represent a sharp decline in real per-student expenditures (see figure 1.1). The effect of the squeeze on resource availability has been exacerbated by inefficiency in resource utilization.

The decrease in resources has been particularly acute in Africa and the Middle East. In Sub-Saharan Africa, during the 1980s average public expenditure per student declined from $6,300 to $1,500 in real terms. In the Middle East and North Africa, it declined from $3,200 to $1,900. In the former socialist countries of Europe and Central Asia, severe declines in resource availability took place in the early 1990s. In Hungary, for example, higher education recurrent expenditures fell by 21 percent from 1991 to 1993. To the extent that it reflects the more efficient use of resources, lower spending per student is desirable, but the quality of higher education teaching and research

FIGURE 1.1 HIGHER EDUCATION ENROLLMENT AND PUBLIC EXPENDITURE ON HIGHER EDUCATION

Average annual percentage growth rate

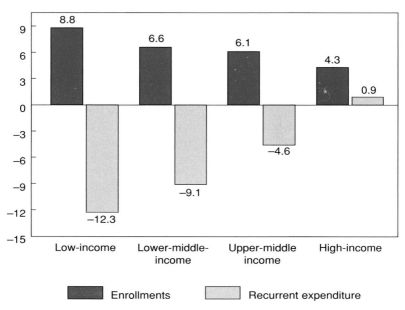

Source: Salmi 1991a.

has deteriorated precipitously in many countries (see box 1.1). Available resources have been stretched beyond minimal levels of effectiveness, indicated by inadequate staffing and deteriorating infrastructure.

Inadequate staffing. Teacher salaries have been declining in real terms and, as a result, the ability of public higher education institutions to retain qualified staff has become a persistent problem in many countries. The more experienced faculty are leaving higher education for better-paying positions elsewhere. More commonly, they devote most of their time to outside work to earn extra income. In Nigeria, for example, public university salaries in 1992 are only 10 percent of their 1978 real value. Because of its unattractive remuneration scheme, the University of Malaysia has been losing its top lecturers to the private sector. In Bulgaria, the 35 percent decline in real

---

BOX 1.1 DECLINING CAPACITY FOR TEACHING AND RESEARCH IN AFRICAN UNIVERSITIES

Uganda's Makerere University and the University of Dakar in Senegal were for many years after independence two of Africa's premier public universities. Today, their facilities have deteriorated and the quality of instruction provided is profoundly threatened—the consequence of political and economic turmoil combined with chronic underfunding and misallocation.

In Uganda, Makerere University and its affiliated institutions account for 94 percent of all university enrollments. University lecturers receive a salary equivalent to just $19 per month. A 1990 survey indicated that 27 senior staff had resigned from the university since 1989, most to take employment elsewhere, and that 48 percent of teaching positions were unfilled. The low salaries have transformed academic work into part-time employment for many staff. In addition, many of the residence halls are accommodating students far in excess of their physical capacity.

The University of Dakar, originally designed for 3,500 students, enrolled nearly 20,000 students in 1991. There has been a gradual decline in the physical infrastructure—facilities, laboratories, libraries, and so on—because of the lack of resources and maintenance. This is most evident in the library, once the largest in the region. The library's central air conditioning system broke down in 1980 and has not yet been repaired, placing the book collection in jeopardy from heat and dust. The University of Dakar spends five times more money every year to buy medicines for its students and their families than it does to purchase books or periodicals for the library.

Sources: World Bank 1992d, 1992e.

teacher salaries during 1991 as a result of the recession has prompted the departure of qualified personnel. In Russia, the present economic crisis has meant reduced funding for all research institutions, leading to the loss of many researchers.

Deteriorating infrastructure. With continued enrollment expansion accompanied by steadily declining real resources, public institutions have become overcrowded. Higher education managers are increasingly concentrating on meeting immediate operating needs and neglecting the maintenance requirements of the physical plant. Instructional and living conditions have deteriorated in many institutions. Examples of infrastructure decay and insufficient pedagogical resources in classrooms, laboratories, and libraries can be found in all regions. A survey of thirty-one Sub-Saharan African countries revealed that the average number of books per student held by university libraries fell from 49 in 1980 to 7 in 1990.

The decline in academic standards in primary and secondary education has also affected the performance of higher education systems.

Internal Efficiency

In virtually all countries, the decline in resources has been compounded by inefficient use. Even though many public facilities are overburdened by students, they are also often underused. For instance, many university libraries are closed evenings and weekends in accordance with civil service regulations. In some countries, the rapid rise in enrollments has led to the proliferation of uneconomically small, specialized institutions characterized by high unit costs and significant duplication in their program offerings. In China, for instance, the number of higher education institutions surged from 392 at the end of the Cultural Revolution to 1,075 in 1989; by 1989, 35 percent of institutions had fewer than 1,000 students. A 1986 study showed that unit costs in such small institutions were 50 percent higher than in institutions with at least 4,000 students. In Central and Eastern Europe, the higher education sector was deliberately fragmented under socialist regimes for reasons of political control.

Low student-staff ratios, high dropout and repetition rates, and low graduation rates also drive up the cost per graduate. In Brazil, for example, student-teacher ratios are very low in the federal universities (7:1) so that undergraduate unit costs are equivalent to about $6,000. In Venezuela, costs per graduate in public universities are seven times higher than in private universities because of the higher repetition and dropout rates. In Cameroon, the cost per liberal arts graduate in public universities is $74,000 because of the high repetition and dropout rates.

In many countries, a large share of the public higher education budget is devoted to noneducational expenditures in support of student grants and subsidized student services. While representing only 6 percent of recurrent expenditures in Asia and 14 percent in OECD countries, student support represents around 11 percent of spending in Central and Eastern Europe and approximately 20 percent of spending in the Middle East, North Africa, and Latin America. In francophone African countries, allowances for noneducational expenses constitute an average of 55 percent of the entire higher education budget, while in anglophone Africa they are 15 percent. These high subsidies to public university students are not only inefficient education investment but also regressive social spending, because students enrolled in higher education in all developing countries are disproportionately from the upper end of the income distribution.

External Efficiency

Two types of external efficiency affect the higher education systems of developing countries: graduate unemployment and declining research output.

Graduate unemployment. Graduate unemployment in developing countries rose sharply during the 1980s and continues to rise. This reflects principally the sluggish growth of aggregate demand for highly skilled labor and the diminished role of the public sector as the main employer of university graduates.

Employment statistics by level of education are not available for most countries, but where statistics exist, they show that the rapid expansion of higher education has often been accompanied by increasing levels of graduate unemployment and underemployment. In Asia, North Africa, and the Middle East, high unemployment for graduates has been recorded in several countries. For example, in Indonesia, the 1990 unemployment rate among degree holders was 12.6 percent. In the Philippines, 1988 unemployment was 6.8 percent among those who completed undergraduate education and 19.1 percent for those with graduate degrees. College graduates have had persistently higher open unemployment rates than those with incomplete primary and secondary education. In Morocco, the proportion of unemployed graduates rose from 3.5 to 7.2 percent between 1985 and 1989. In Egypt, unemployment among university graduates rose from 9.6 percent in 1976 to 16 percent in 1986, as the government policy of absorbing all graduates in the public sector became unsustainable, and in Jordan, unemployment among higher education graduates was 16.5 percent in 1991. Many Latin American and African countries have experienced similar trends. In Venezuela, for instance, the proportion of unemployed university graduates increased from 4 percent in 1981 to 10 percent in 1990.

Graduate unemployment is likely to worsen in the near and medium terms since, in many countries, economic stagnation is adversely affecting the economy's capacity to absorb the rapidly growing numbers of higher education graduates. In Africa, the pursuit of economic stabilization and adjustment programs will amplify the slowdown of public sector employment growth—which has traditionally been the main outlet for university graduates—and it will take time for the private sector to become the main provider of employment. In the former socialist countries of Central and Eastern Europe, the transition to a market economy has been marked by large cuts in the number of jobs in state-owned enterprises and a rapid rise in unemployment, though this period should be followed by one of increased private sector employment.

In many countries, the problem of graduate unemployment is compounded by government policies that create serious labor market distortions, inflating the private returns from higher education. High entry wages determined by civil service regulations and, in some countries (such as Egypt and Yemen in the past), guaranteed public sector employment for university graduates are examples of such distortions. In addition, subsidization of university studies has contributed to making higher education economically attractive, even when jobs are not readily available in the wider economy after graduation. Unless such policies are accompanied by strict rationing mechanisms, unplanned and fiscally unsustainable growth in enrollment is an inevitable outcome.

Where government policies determine the size and distribution of student intake, the allocation of students to different fields of study may have little to do with market demand or individual aptitudes. In many African countries, the majority of students are enrolled in the arts and humanities, because these have traditionally led to government employment, and very few students pursue natural sciences and engineering programs. In the former socialist countries of Europe and Asia, on the contrary, enrollments in applied scientific fields are far higher than in other programs because of priority given by former East Bloc countries to building scientific expertise. In Romania, for example, more than two-thirds of all university enrollments are in engineering and technical training programs, and there is currently a dearth of qualified people with training in the social sciences and management to support the transition to a market economy.

Declining research output. In most developing countries, universities usually account for a significant proportion of national research expenditures and employ the bulk of scientists engaged in research and development work. However, many countries have failed to utilize their potential for advanced scientific training and research. The majority of African countries, which have relatively small scientific communities, have been unable to support national research efforts and, in some cases, experienced severe erosion of their capacity to offer training in scientific and technological fields. For example, between 1977 and 1987, mainstream scientific output declined by 67 percent in Ghana and 53 percent in Uganda, as measured by the number of scientific publications in national and international journals. Declines in output also took place in Angola, Ethiopia, Mozambique, the Sudan, and Zimbabwe.

In many Latin American countries, including Argentina, Brazil, and Mexico, where most research activity takes place in public scientific institutions, university research has had very little impact on the economy. Most Latin American universities are essentially teaching institutions, and their research is rarely intended for practical applications, reflecting the traditionally low level of university-industry interaction. Moreover, in recent years state funding for research and development has been declining, as has private investment in research and development.

When Eastern and Central Europe were under communist regimes, the separation of scientific research from advanced scientific training was a major obstacle to their ability to contribute to the economy. Since the revolution of the late 1980s, resources supporting government scientific institutions have also diminished, and the long-term viability of these countries' training and research systems is seriously compromised. Between 1985 and 1988, the number of publications in the former USSR declined by 10 percent. In the former Czechoslovakia this number declined by 13 percent, in Hungary by 7 percent, and in Romania by 38 percent.

Only in the newly industrialized economies of Southeast Asia has the scientific output of universities significantly increased. In the Republic of Korea and Singapore, contributions to mainstream research grew 609 percent and 143 percent respectively between 1971 and 1985. Between 1985 and 1988 in China the number of publications increased by 75 percent, in Taiwan (China) by 76 percent, in Korea by 56 percent, and in Thailand by 28 percent. Korea has been particularly successful in supporting local technological innovations, relying on grants to universities and research centers to foster joint research projects.

Equity

The rapid growth of enrollments has led to increased access to higher education for traditionally less privileged populations, including women and students of rural origin. Teacher training colleges, in particular, have been instrumental in ensuring a fairer geographic, ethnic, and income distribution of higher education enrollments.

However, higher education is still very elitist. Although few countries collect data on the socioeconomic origin of students, household survey data clearly indicate that the majority of students come from wealthier families. For example, in Latin America, white-collar employees make up only 15 percent of the population, but their children account for 45 percent of higher education enrollments. In francophone Africa, white-collar employees represent only 6 percent of the total labor force, but this group accounts for 40 percent of enrollments. In South Africa, white students comprise about 80 percent of university enrollments, whereas only 13 percent of the total population is white. Professionals make up about 10 percent of the populations of Asia and the Middle East, but their children represent 43 percent and 47 percent of higher education enrollments, respectively. A principal reason that attendance at tertiary institutions, especially those institutions with the best instruction and finest reputations, remains heavily biased in favor of students from wealthy families is that children from poorer families have much more limited access to good quality primary and secondary education.

Since higher education systems are financed by the entire population but available only to a small minority, they have a regressive fiscal impact. In Brazil, 23 percent of the public education budget goes to higher education, even though higher education represents only 2 percent of the student population and draws disproportionately from the highest-income families. Similarly, in Rwanda 15 percent of the budget goes to 0.2 percent of the student population. In Morocco, only 5 percent of young people eventually obtain university degrees, but those in this fortunate minority receive 35 percent of total government expenditures on education.

Despite the fact that female enrollment rates have grown faster than male enrollment rates, women are still sorely underrepresented in higher education in many countries. While male and female enrollment ratios are relatively equal in the former socialist countries of Eastern and Central Europe and in some Latin American countries (for example, Brazil), in 1989 women accounted for only 25 percent of enrollments in Africa, 35 percent in Asia, 36 percent in the Middle East and North Africa, and 47 percent in Latin America and the Caribbean.

Even in countries where women form a higher proportion of the student body, they tend to be disproportionately enrolled in non-university institutions. For example, in Lesotho, where women are 63 percent of total tertiary enrollments, they account for only 49 percent of university enrollments; in Poland, where women represent 58 percent of all tertiary enrollments, they are 50 percent of university students. In Argentina, women account for 53 percent of higher education students but only 46 percent of university students.

In addition, women continue to be concentrated in traditionally "female" fields such as nursing, teaching, and the clerical professions. In Chile, for example, only 6 percent of engineering students are women, compared with 61 percent of education students and 90 percent of nursing students. In Bangladesh, females constitute 2 percent of enrollments in engineering, as compared with 63 percent in education and the humanities. In Korea, the figures are 2 and 52 percent, respectively. By contrast, in Europe the average proportion of female students in engineering programs is more than 15 percent.

A major determinant of gender inequality in higher education is low female participation at the primary and secondary levels. Factors such as family income and traditional attitudes toward women only amplify the problem at the tertiary level. Another issue is the gender streaming that occurs in secondary education. Particularly serious is the low proportion of females receiving advanced science instruction at the senior secondary level. This is often the result of lack of positive exposure to science and technology in primary and lower secondary education. The poor representation of females in science programs at the university level reflects the smaller proportion of girls eligible for entry. Sometimes it reveals as well the impact of distorted labor markets. When women are aware of labor market discrimination and denied entry into prestigious occupations, most choose to graduate from fields where such barriers do not exist. Conversely, when women are restricted to "female" fields of study, they do not acquire the qualifications necessary to compete in the open labor market. Their education is geared to a small number of occupations in the social sectors, where there are fewer prospects for advancement and where salaries are lower. The exclusion of a large proportion of women from higher education is not only inequitable; it also reduces economic efficiency and growth.

Underrepresentation of women results in a waste of talent. In the University of Indonesia, for example, female students outperformed male students. Holding test scores and the department of enrollment constant, women's grade point average was about 0.35 higher than men (on a scale of 4). In the case of Mauritius, women also outperformed men. Ninety-eight percent of women passed the diploma level examination, compared with 86 percent of men, and 94 percent of women passed the degree examination, compared with 81 percent of men. These examples illustrate that increasing the representation of women could bring about a gain in the quality of students admitted to institutions of higher education.

Strategies for Reform

The bleak economic outlook makes it unlikely that public financing for higher education will increase significantly in this decade. Yet in many countries, for political and social reasons, governments have committed themselves to expansionary policies aimed at accommodating the growing demand for higher education, often without reference to available resources, quality standards, and labor market demands and at little or no direct cost to students. Unless reforms are implemented to improve the performance of higher education, many countries are destined to enter the twenty-first century insufficiently prepared to compete in the global economy, where growth will be based ever more heavily on technical and scientific knowledge. But in many countries, strong student activism and weak governments have prevented the introduction of critically needed reform.

A number of OECD countries have responded to the funding crisis by introducing innovative policies during the past decade aimed at increasing higher education efficiency (such as the Netherlands' use of funding formulas) and stimulating greater private funding (as in Australia and Ireland). Despite the relentless fiscal pressures that most developing countries face, few have made significant progress in the area of higher education reform. Yet the experience of a few developing countries such as Chile indicates that it is possible to achieve a well-functioning, diversified, and growing higher education system even as public spending per student declines.

Indeed, it is arguable that higher education should not have the highest priority claim on incremental public resources available for education in many developing countries, especially those that have not yet achieved adequate access, equity, and quality at the primary and secondary levels. This is because of the priority that countries attach to achieving universal literacy; because the social rates of return to investments in primary and secondary education usually exceed the social returns to higher education; and because investments in basic education can improve equity because they tend to reduce income inequalities.

Each country needs to weigh carefully the right balance of resource allocation between the three education subsectors, considering the relative social rates of return at each level as well as the complementarity which exists between primary, secondary, and tertiary education. For example, the quality of higher education is determined by the quality of primary and secondary students. Higher education specialists participate in curriculum design and educational research for lower levels. The training of teachers and school administrators is carried out at the tertiary level. Furthermore, the overwhelming fiscal reality in most developing countries is such that quality improvements and enrollment expansion in higher education will have to be achieved with little or no increase in public expenditures.

Having documented the depth of the higher education crisis, particularly in the public sector, this study now analyzes the lessons of experience to show how developing countries can achieve the goals of greater efficiency, quality, and equity in higher education. A review of country experience identifies four key directions for reform that can help countries achieve these goals without increased public funding. These are:

- Encouraging greater differentiation of institutions, including the development of private institutions (chapter 2)
- Providing incentives for public institutions to diversify sources of funding, including cost-sharing with students, and linking government funding closely to performance (chapter 3)
- Redefining the role of government in higher education (chapter 4)
- Introducing policies explicitly designed to give priority to quality and equity objectives (chapter 5).

Chapter 6 examines the experience of the World Bank in supporting higher education and summarizes the lessons that the Bank is increasingly putting into practice to support countries in reforming higher education so as to achieve greater quality, efficiency, and equity.

In no country will achieving these reforms be easy. As discussed above, the predominant pattern of public higher education in the developing world principally benefits the most affluent households, which are also the most powerful politically. The children of the well-off are heavily subsidized by the rest of society to attend public universities, reinforcing their economic and social advantage. Experience demonstrates that breaking this pattern is essential, and also that the political difficulty of doing so should not be underestimated. In countries with fragile systems of governance, students with grievances—and there will be grievances if subsidies and privileges are reduced—can represent a threat to political stability. Governments therefore necessarily tread warily in introducing reforms that affect the most powerful households and those with the potential to destabilize political regimes.

Reform requirements and political and economic conditions vary considerably across regions, however, and there is no single blueprint appropriate for every country. While the four main areas of the report constitute broad directions for reform, the pace of reform implementation and the relative importance of various options will obviously depend on specific country circumstances such as the pattern of economic growth, the level of income, and the degree of education development (for example, primary- and secondary-level coverage, and the existence of private institutions in various education subsectors). Each country must therefore develop the policy framework that best fits its particular circumstances. This book draws lessons from a wide range of country and institutional experiences from both the industrial and developing worlds. A review of these experiences reveals many clear differences but, at the same time, also some convergence in regard to the principal features of successful higher education reform programs. This book is intended to capture the commonalities as well as the differences, in order to inform the process of policy analysis and policy choice in countries intent on improving the equity, efficiency, and quality of their higher education systems.

The Growing Diversity of Institutions

THE TRADITIONAL model of the European research university, with its one-tier program structure, has proven expensive and inappropriate to meet the multiple demands of economic and social development as well as the learning needs of a more diverse student body. Increased differentiation in higher education, that is, the development of non-university institutions and the growth of private institutions, can help meet the growing social demand for higher education and make higher education systems more responsive to changing labor market needs. The decisions by which countries manage the pace and pattern of enrollment growth through increased differentiation affect significantly the amount of public resources available to finance higher education. Some countries have succeeded in this regard, developing a range of institutions with a variety of missions, such as short-cycle programs and open learning systems, and promoting private institutions to complement the public network. A recent study (Tan and Mingat 1992, p. 11) observed that:

> The achievement of Asian education becomes all the more remarkable when levels of government spending on education are compared across regions. Expressed as a percentage of GNP, governments in Asia spend less on education than governments in all other regions. This apparent paradox—high coverage despite relatively little fiscal effort—gives a first indication that as a determinant of education development, public policies in the sector are at least as important as the size of public spending.

Differentiating Institutional Missions

Higher education systems may be classified into three broad categories according to the degree of institutional differentiation: (1) an undifferentiated public or "university-based" system, which consists only of public universities; (2) a "differentiated public" system, which consists only of public institutions but includes a significant number of non-university tertiary institutions as well as universities; and (3) a "differentiated public plus private" system, which has both public and private institutions.

As illustrated by figure 2.1, the degree of diversification tends to increase with country income. Among low-income nations, higher education systems are entirely public "university-based" in 61 percent of the cases; in this income group 26 percent of countries belong to the "differentiated public"

FIGURE 2.1 DEGREE OF DIFFERENTIATION OF HIGHER EDUCATION SYSTEMS BY INCOME LEVEL

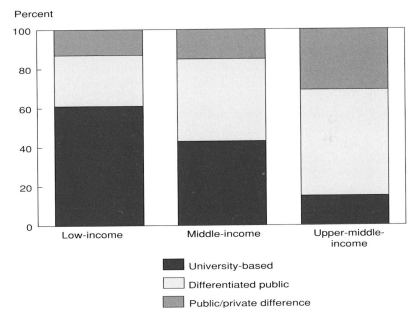

Source: World Bank estimates.

category and only 13 percent to the "public/private differentiated" group. By contrast, in the upper-middle-income group, only 15 percent of countries are purely "university-based," 54 percent have "differentiated public" systems, and 31 percent have differentiated systems with both public and private institutions.

Among all world regions, Asia is the continent where differentiation efforts have been the most extensive and most effective. Thailand, for example, has established two open universities and several regional universities to augment Bangkok's four prestigious national universities. China has set up a network of provincial universities and a television university for distance education. India has 3 million part-time students enrolled in correspondence courses, along with its 4 million regular full-time students. Indonesia, the Republic of Korea, and the Philippines have relied heavily on the private higher education sector to accommodate most of the social demand for tertiary education.

In the Middle East and North Africa, Jordan displays the most institutional variety. In Jordan, 52 percent of the total student population is enrolled in public and private community colleges or in teacher training institutes. In Africa, where most higher education systems consist predominantly of public universities, Nigeria and Kenya stand out as the countries with the most differentiation in their higher education systems. Besides the 21 federal universities, Nigeria has 8 state universities, 1 military university, 31 polytechnics, 45 colleges of education, and 33 other higher education institutions. In Kenya, 3 national polytechnics and 11 private colleges operate alongside the public universities and teacher training institutions.

In Latin America, the differentiation of higher education has been driven by the growth of private institutions. This is especially true in Chile and Brazil. Until 1980, Chile had only a few universities (two public and six private). But a major higher education reform implemented in the early 1980s has brought about the establishment of 82 professional institutes (PIs), 168 two-year technical centers (TCs), and the division of the two national universities into 12 smaller ones. Enrollments in higher education have doubled as a result, with most of the expansion occurring in non-university private institutions (PIs and TCs). During the same period, the share of public expenditures on higher education in GDP declined from 1.65 percent to 0.45 percent. Brazil has 21 federal universities, 13 state universities, 5 municipal universities, and 61 private universities, in addition to a large number of state and private non-university institutions.

In a number of Eastern and Central European countries, the situation that prevailed before the democratic revolution of the late 1980s was one of institutional fragmentation, where a large number of small, narrowly specialized, uncoordinated institutions operated under many different government authorities. In recent years, attempts have been made to consolidate the various networks of higher education institutions and to provide a viable legal and policy framework for the increasingly differentiated higher education programs and institutions needed to meet the challenge of the transition to a market economy.

Developing Non-University Institutions

During the last two decades, enrollments in non-university institutions, both public and private, have grown faster than in traditional universities. In East Asia, for example, the average annual growth of university enrollments was 11 percent between 1975 and 1980 and 6 percent between 1980 and 1988, as compared with 24 and 10 percent for non-university institutions in the same periods. Several types of non-university institutions have evolved in various countries, for example, polytechnics, short-cycle professional and technical institutes, community colleges, and institutions offering distance education and adult education programs.

The principal advantages of such institutions include lower program costs, which reflect shorter courses, lower dropout rates, and lower per-student annual expenditures. In Tunisia, for example, a network of two-year technology institutes has recently been established. The lower cost per graduate is expected to bring about an overall 12 percent decrease in the average cost of higher education graduates in the country. In Ghana, unit costs at non-university institutions, such as the diploma-awarding colleges, are only 40 percent of the average cost of university education. In the Pacific Islands, the unit costs of technical institutions in agriculture, marine studies, and nursing are between 30 and 50 percent of unit costs at the University of the South Pacific. A similar pattern exists in Bulgaria, which has a three-tier system of higher education (universities, higher institutes, and technical institutes). Average costs at the universities are 15 percent more than at the higher institutes and 95 percent more than at the technical institutes. The technical institutes account for only 10 percent of the higher education budget, but they enroll almost 20 percent of post-secondary students.

Many non-university institutions offer training opportunities that respond flexibly to labor market demand rather than supply-side factors. In Brazil, for example, the Technology Centers of SENAI (National Industrial Training Services) operate multi-disciplinary programs in various technical fields. As Poland moves toward a market economy, the government is setting up five short-cycle institutes of technology on the assumption that such institutions are more likely than traditional university programs to produce the types of skilled labor demanded in a market economy. In Singapore, the employment prospects for graduates of polytechnics are so good that many talented students seek entry into the vocationally oriented polytechnics rather than the regular academic programs offered by the universities.

In the engineering education field, a new distinction has appeared between "engineering scientists" and "applied engineers." The former are involved in more analytical and abstract work, whereas jobs filled by the latter focus on production processes. The new programs in applied engineering, which are typically offered in polytechnics and equivalent institutions, stress a broad spectrum of engineering applications in production, manufacturing, and testing. They are complemented by engineering technology programs in two- or three-year institutions at the diploma or associate degree level. These institutions include community colleges, colleges of applied arts and technology, and technology institutes. In the developing world, Mexico is an example of a country that has established an extensive network of technology institutes with a more applied focus.

Non-university institutions help meet the demand for improved access to higher education by minority groups and underprivileged students. For example, women's colleges and polytechnics such as the ones established in Bangladesh and India respond to the educational needs of girls in small towns and rural areas. In India, while all the Industrial Training Institutes (ITIs) enroll women, 132 separate women's ITIs have been established to encourage women to obtain vocational training. Initially, training was offered in the largely "female" occupations such as tailoring, dress designing, hairdressing, and cooking. But these programs have been redesigned to address the needs of modern industry, and subjects such as electronics, computer science, systems control, and instrumentation increasingly attract female applicants. Teacher training colleges and technical training institutions, which are the most localized in their recruitment and mission, are in many countries effective in increasing participation by educationally and economically disadvantaged groups.

However, two risks have to be considered in the development of non-university institutions. First, when such institutions are perceived to be second-rate, there is a risk of student discontent, as has developed in countries where the public technical institutes are underfunded and become dead-end institutions serving as "academic parking lots" for surplus students. In Egypt, which has one of the largest higher education systems in the developing world, the government has addressed the social demand issue by restricting access to the thirteen universities and creating a network of two-year post-secondary technical institutes for secondary graduates who do not qualify for the universities. The technical institutes have expanded rapidly during the last fifteen years and now enroll about 40 percent of those leaving the secondary schools, but the financial, human, and material resources needed to sustain good-quality programs have not been forthcoming. As a result, the quality of learning is low and graduates cannot find good jobs.

Second, there is a risk of "academic drift" associated with the development of non-university institutions. There have been numerous instances of non-university institutions being diverted from their original academic mission and being upgraded gradually to full-fledged universities, thus defeating the purpose of providing alternative educational opportunities. In Egypt, for example, Helwan University was founded in 1975 by combining several technical institutes into a university. Between 1968 and 1975, the programs at Helwan Higher Institute of Technology were based on the German model of the "Fachhochschule" (a specialized technical institute) and received support from the Federal Republic of Germany. But the lack of academic and professional recognition by the Supreme Council of Universities and the Syndicate of Egyptian Engineers put pressure on the Helwan Institute to transform itself into a full degree-granting university. The recent abolition of the distinction between universities and polytechnics in the United Kingdom is a manifestation of a similar trend among British polytechnics.

Distance education and open learning programs can be effective in increasing access, at modest cost, for underprivileged groups that are usually poorly represented in university enrollments. In India, 41 percent of the students enrolled in open universities and other distance education programs are women, compared with only 32 percent in formal university programs. Distance education can be an effective way also to provide lifelong education and upgrade skills, as when used for in-service teacher training. In the last two decades, distance education has rapidly expanded in Bangladesh, China, India, Indonesia, Korea, Pakistan, the Philippines, Sri Lanka, and Thailand. Thailand's two open universities, Ramkhambaeng and Sukhothai Thammathirat, have been the government's principal instrument for expanding access to students from the poorest social strata, especially in urban areas. Operating on a self-financing basis, the open universities account for 62 percent of Thailand's higher education enrollments. Distance education programs can also be designed with a regional (multinational) clientele. For example, UNISA, the Open University of South Africa, draws 15,000 of its 120,000 students from neighboring countries.

Distance education programs are usually much less expensive than conventional university programs, given the higher student-teacher ratios (see table 2.1). In Thailand, for instance, the average ratio is 8:1 in the selective public universities, compared to 745:1 in the open universities. To appreciate the relative merits of open universities and conventional institutions, it would also be useful to compare labor market outcomes, but comparative data on this aspect are generally not available.

Private institutions are an important element of some of the strongest higher education systems to be found today in developing countries. They can respond efficiently and flexibly to changing demands of students and changing labor market conditions. Furthermore, private provision of higher education increases educational opportunities at little or no direct public cost, especially in countries where public institutions are very selective. Governments can encourage the development of private higher education to complement public institutions as a means of managing the cost of expanding higher education enrollments, increasing the diversity of training programs, and broadening social participation in higher education. In a number of countries, the majority of students are enrolled in private higher education institutions: for example, 86 percent in the Philippines, 75 percent in Korea, and 60 percent in Bangladesh, Brazil, Colombia, and Indonesia (see figure 2.2). In these coun-

TABLE 2.1 DISTANCE UNIVERSITIES IN ASIA: COST AND EFFECTIVENESS DATA

Country and institution	Type of cost	Cost/student		(1)/(2), in percent	Measure used	Rate, in percent
		Distance (1)	Conventional (2)			
Thailand; STOU	average cost per graduate	B 7,023	B 49,957	14.1	Percent dropouts	50
Pakistan; AIOU	average cost per student 1988 est.	Rs 4,585	Rs 20,960	21.9	Mean rate of dropouts for all courses	42.5
China; CRTVU	average cost per student 1981	Y 1,000	Y 2,000	50.0	Percent graduated in 1982 from 1979 enrollees	69
Rep. of Korea; KACU	total cost per student per year 1981	US$125	US$1,250	10.0	Percent dropouts after first year of study	50

Note: STOU: Sukhothai Thammathirat Open University; AIOU: Allama Iqbal Open University; CRTVU: Chinese Radio and Television University; KACU: Korea Air and Correspondence University.
Source: Lockheed, Middleton, and Nettleton 1991.

FIGURE 2.2 SHARE OF ENROLLMENT IN PRIVATE HIGHER EDUCATION
(percent)

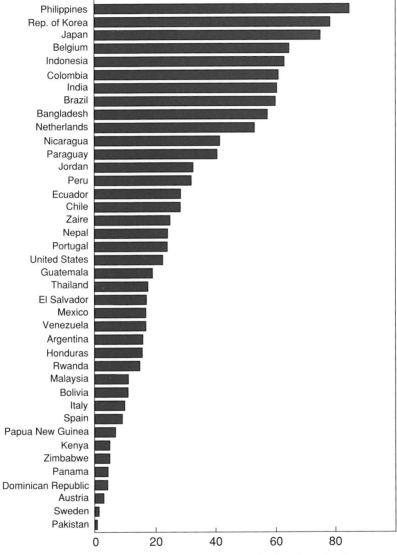

Note: In the few Western European countries which have a high proportion of enrollments in private institutions (for example, Belgium and the Netherlands), higher education continues to be almost entirely financed by the state which subsidizes both public and private higher education institutions.

Source: World Bank data.

tries, access to higher education has been substantially broadened without imposing an unsustainable financial burden on the government budget.

There is often greater variation of quality within the private sector than between public and private institutions. On the one hand, private universities are among the top universities in several countries, such as Colombia, Peru, and the Philippines. On the other hand, the quality of training at many private institutions, which tend to offer programs in a limited number of disciplines where teaching costs are relatively low (such as accounting or law, compared with physics or medicine), is less than satisfactory. For instance, in the Philippines, differences have been observed between private nonprofit and for-profit colleges and universities. The nonprofit institutions are typically smaller and more selective and have higher private costs than the for-profits. In addition, graduates from the nonprofit institutions eventually get higher-paying jobs than graduates from proprietary institutions, reflecting the better quality of those institutions as perceived by employers.

Furthermore, the expansion of private higher education in the absence of cost recovery in the public sector and loan or grant programs for the poor can produce a double inequity. The most privileged students move from the best (often private) secondary schools into free public universities, while the poorer students end up paying for the lesser-quality education offered by private tertiary institutions. In Thailand, 74 percent of the students attending the best public universities come from middle- and upper-income families, and the fees paid by students represent only 7 percent of recurrent costs at these elite institutions. In Brazil's federal universities, which charge no tuition, 44 percent of students come from families in the top 10 percent of the income distribution, whereas only 18 percent come from families in the bottom half of the income distribution. Unless cost-sharing is also introduced in public universities, diversity and equity objectives cannot be effectively served by the growth of private higher education.

The lack of an appropriate legal and policy framework can impede the growth of private higher education (see box 2.1). Recent experience in Kenya has shown that the contribution of private higher education is most positive when the government creates a basic and consistent regulatory framework that allows the private higher education sector to flourish. Such a framework avoids restrictive regulations which suffocate private initiatives—such as the prohibition that some countries still maintain on the provision of private higher education. Policies to encourage private higher education involve establishing appropriate accreditation and program evaluation mechanisms, providing technical assistance for curriculum development and institutional management, avoiding disincentives such as tuition price controls and, sometimes, offering financial incentives to support the development and qualitative improvement of private higher education institutions. For example, the new Higher Education Law in Colombia (December 1992) provides for an accreditation system for both public and private institutions. In several countries (for example, Chile and Colombia), admission to both public and private higher education institutions is determined by a national examination, and merit scholarships are available to students attending both types of institutions. This provides incentives to public and private institutions alike to compete on the basis of quality.

The availability of public subsidies is an important factor in explaining the growth of private higher education in countries such as Indonesia, Japan, Korea, the Philippines, and Thailand. In Indonesia, for example, private higher education institutions receive significant subsidies through the assignment of some staff in government service to teach in these institutions. The development of private institutions can also be fostered through tax exemptions (Brazil, Mexico), direct monetary grants (Chile and India), and subsidized land grants (Iran, Kenya, and Uganda) (see box 2.2). This, however, is not an

---

BOX 2.1 PRIVATE HIGHER EDUCATION IN FORMER SOCIALIST COUNTRIES: THE NEED FOR AN APPROPRIATE LEGAL AND POLICY FRAMEWORK

A nascent private sector exists in Central and Eastern Europe, but its growth is impeded by the lack of an appropriate legal and policy framework. Hungary, Bulgaria, the Czech Republic, Poland, Romania, and the Slovak Republic are all exploring private initiatives. Given that public sector financing will be significantly decreasing at the very time that these countries are trying to "catch up with the rest of Europe" in terms of the proportion of the age cohort enrolled in higher education, private institutions and private financing can play a critical role. One example of private initiative is the City University in Bratislava, modeled after the public Open University in the United King-

dom. In Poland, besides the prestigious Catholic University of Lublin, which has been in existence for a long time, five new private higher education institutions have recently started to operate. In Romania, about sixty private higher education institutions have recently been established, offering courses in commerce, computer science, and foreign languages, with a total enrollment of more than 80,000 students. However, many fail after only a few months because of poor management and undercapitalization. The development of private higher education institutions is constrained in the region by the absence of a legal framework for recognition, accreditation, and certification, although Hungary and Romania have made such provisions in pending education laws.

Source: Richards 1992a.

BOX 2.2 IRAN'S ISLAMIC AZAD UNIVERSITY

Iran's Islamic Azad University (IAU), a privately financed, nonprofit institution founded in 1983, is possibly the largest private higher education enterprise in the world. By all measures, the institution has experienced spectacular growth during the past ten years. Student enrollments have increased from 2,500 to more than 300,000, degree programs from 10 to 126, and the number of campuses from 9 to 116, located in 105 cities. In addition, a dynamic construction program is underway: 70 of 116 campuses are currently engaged in construction projects, of which 30 involve brand new integrated campuses designed to house some 15,000 to 50,000 students each.

IAU students now represent some 40 percent of total higher education enrollments in the country, while the remaining 60 percent attend the public, tuition-free system. Remarkably, this has been achieved without state support for recurrent expenditures, most of which are covered by student tuition. The state has helped the university's capital development by providing land and building grants during campus start-up; private donations from local businesses and civic groups have also been instrumental.

The rapid expansion, however, coupled with the quasi-exclusive reliance on student tuition for recurrent spending, has also led to some qualitative deficiencies: only 14 percent of faculty are full-time, laboratories and libraries lack basic provisions, and central management tools are weak or nonexistent. The university's current long-term development plan, with its increased emphasis on educational quality enhancement, aims at redressing these deficiencies.

Source: Islamic Azad University 1992.

argument for subsidizing the private sector. Financial incentives to stimulate the development of private institutions can only be justified on the grounds that they provide a means of expanding enrollments at lower public cost than by expanding public institutions.

Income from student tuition fees frequently accounts for a very high proportion of the recurrent budgets of private institutions in developing countries, much higher than in many private institutions in industrialized economies. Since demand for private schooling in developing countries tends to be very price- and income-elastic, it can be difficult for private institutions to improve instructional facilities, offer new high-cost programs of study, or increase the proportion of full-time staff without altering the socioeconomic selectivity or the size of enrollments. Governments can help in two ways. First, private institutions must be allowed to set their own fees and exercise a substantial measure of autonomy in determining the composition of their student bodies and the types of academic programs they offer. Second, government loans and scholarships can be made available to financially needy students attending private institutions. All other capital grants, research funding, and other financial support for quality improvements can be made equally available to public and private institutions on the basis of the quality of their proposals. This serves the long-term objective of establishing a level playing field for all higher education institutions, public and private alike, using competition for public resources as a stimulus for improved quality and increased efficiency, as has been done in Brazil and Korea with a competitive peer review process for research funding, and in Chile with the merit scholarship program.

CHAPTER THREE

Diversifying the Funding of Public Institutions and Introducing Incentives for Their Performance

IN ALL countries, public institutions will continue to educate a large share, if not the majority, of students even if the role of the private sector is strengthened and most *new* enrollments are channeled into private institutions. Experience shows that if public institutions are to achieve higher quality and greater efficiency, governments will need to implement sweeping reforms in financing designed to:

- Mobilize greater private financing for public higher education

- Provide support to qualified students unable to pursue advanced studies for reasons of inadequate family income

- Foster efficiency in allocating and utilizing resources among and within public institutions.

Mobilizing Greater Private Financing

There are several main ways in which governments can mobilize greater private financing: cost-sharing with students, raising funds from alumni and external sources, and engaging in other income-generating activities.

Cost-Sharing with Students

The financial base of public higher education can be strengthened by mobilizing a greater share of the necessary financing from students themselves, who can expect significantly greater lifetime earnings as a result of attending higher education institutions and who often come from families with ample ability to contribute to the costs of higher education. Cost-sharing can be pursued by charging tuition fees in public institutions and eliminating subsidies for noninstructional costs. Governments can permit public institutions to establish their own tuition and fees without interference. Governments can focus on providing prospective students with objective information about school quality. Countries can also eliminate all subsidization of noninstructional expenditures such as housing and meals.

A growing number of developing countries are moving in the direction of cost-sharing (see figure 3.1). Income from student fees in public universities is 22 percent of recurrent expenditures in Viet Nam, 36 percent in Chile, 40 percent in Jordan, and 46 percent in the Republic of Korea. Singapore, which has increased tuition gradually since 1986 and substantially since 1989, now has a policy of automatic 5–7 percent annual increases in student tuition fees to keep pace with wage and other cost increases. In China, as a result of a new student funding system in place since 1989, tuition for regular students is set at about 9 percent of unit costs. However, self-supported students—those admitted on a lower entrance examination score than that required for regular subsidized students—pay tuition fees ten times higher than regular students, fully covering instructional costs. In Hungary, tuition fees are being introduced for students who do not obtain high marks. In Botswana and Ghana, subsidies for student meals have been eliminated, the catering function privatized, and significant cost savings have been achieved.

At present, tuition fees account for more than 10 percent of recurrent expenditures for public higher education in only 20 countries. The importance of fees is not directly related to the income level of a country. The proportion of countries with significant cost recovery in public institutions is relatively the same for low-income (13 percent), lower-middle-income (17 percent), and upper-middle-income groups (15 percent). However, there is variation across regions. Sub-Saharan Africa, North Africa, the Middle East, and Eastern Europe have little or no tradition of cost recovery in public higher education. The situation is quite different in the Latin American and, especially, Asian regions. In one out of five Latin American countries and in half of all Asian countries public institutions charge tuition that generates, on average, more than 10 percent of recurrent expenditures in public higher education.

FIGURE 3.1 TUITION FEES AS A PROPORTION OF RECURRENT EXPENDITURES IN PUBLIC
HIGHER EDUCATION INSTITUTIONS
(percent)

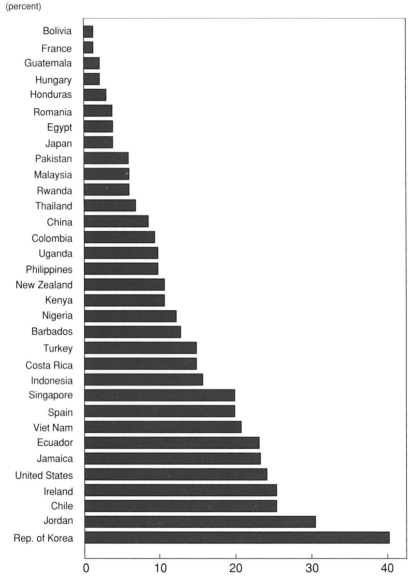

Source: World Bank estimates.

Funding from Alumni and External Sources

A second strategy for diversifying the financial base of public higher education is mobilization of donations and endowments from alumni and private industry. These contributions, essentially gifts to the universities, can take many forms, including funding for the construction of new facilities, the endowment of professorial chairs, donations of scientific equipment, books and art, or provision of scholarships for needy students. The University of the West Indies, for example, recently convened its first alumni conference and obtained $600,000 in pledges to support capital investments and establish a scholarship fund. Firms or government ministries sometimes offer bonded scholarships, for which the recipients are obliged to work for the firm after graduation. In Chile, Indonesia, Thailand, and Venezuela, private industry provides scholarships or subsidized loans for talented students, usually near the completion of their studies.

This kind of philanthropy is frequently a response to tax regimes that encourage such donations. Tax incentives in Chile, for example, give private companies a tax exemption on 50 percent of their donations to universities. India is the developing country with the most generous tax concessions on philanthropic contributions to universities: 150 percent of individual and corporate contributions are tax deductible. While this has prompted a significant increase in donations, particularly in the endowment of professorial chairs, income from donations remains modest in relation to total university expenditures (only 0.6 percent).

The establishment of trust funds with initial support from the external aid and lending community can be a useful form of endowment, especially in small states with a limited economic base. The University of the South Pacific, for example, recently received a Japanese grant designed to finance a particular university department for a fixed period and, at the same time, build up an investment fund that would generate enough revenue to support the department beyond the project's end.

Income-Generating Activities

A third strategy for public institutions is the pursuit of income-generating activities such as short vocational courses, contract research for industry, and consultancy services. Governments can encourage this, and particularly can avoid the *disincentive* of reducing government budget allocations to public institutions to offset incremental resources raised by the institutions from outside sources. Positive incentives could include government matching funds linked to outside income in some ratio or the inclusion of income generated from outside sources as a positive element in funding formulas. Among the ways in which higher education institutions can generate income are short-term training courses and contract research.

Short-term training courses. Short-term instruction courses for enterprises or individuals, organized to complement regular teaching and research activities, can generate significant revenues. They can provide additional income to staff, generate additional revenues for the universities and colleges, and provide market-relevant skills for the economy. In Viet Nam, for instance, the transition to a market economy has created a large demand for short-term courses that upgrade skills: virtually all universities and colleges now offer English language programs and most sponsor night courses in computers and information technology. A recent survey indicated that Vietnamese universities now receive about 8 percent of their revenue from these sources.

Contract research. Contract research can include business services and economic studies for government and private industry, in addition to applied scientific and technological research. Separate legal and management structures are often employed to ensure efficient provision of services. This is the case of the Korean Advanced Institute for Science and Technology, which provides such services under separate management. Public higher education institutions can also be encouraged to seek additional outside funds by matching grants. In Singapore, for example, the government matches private research grants won by higher education institutions.

The Scope for Funding Diversification

In virtually all developing countries, if public higher education institutions wish to increase their overall level of financing or improve their financial stability, mobilizing a greater share of their revenues from nongovernment sources will be essential. Even those countries which devote a significant share of national budgetary resources to higher education can rarely avoid year-to-year fluctuations in funding, which can make it very difficult for institutions to manage their activities efficiently. Eliminating noninstructional subsidies, introducing (or increasing) fees, pursuing donations, and undertaking income-generating activities will provide institutions with a more diversified and stable funding base. An indicative target could be for public higher education institutions to generate income covering about 30 percent of their total recurrent expenditure requirements from nongovernment sources. This is reasonable, given that several countries have already achieved this percentage with tuition fees alone. The time required to reach this target will vary with country circumstances, however, and countries such as Chile, Jordan, and Korea that have already achieved this degree of resource diversification may well want to go further. In addition to reducing their dependence on public financing and their vulnerability to budget fluctuations, the active mobilization of funds from the private sector makes institutions more responsive to market signals. Cost-sharing with students also creates important incentives for students to select their programs of study carefully and to minimize their time in school.

The marginal benefits of revenues obtained through fees and other income-generating activities that institutions can themselves control can be very high, especially in countries where budgetary support transferred by the government is largely or fully absorbed by salaries. If the incremental resources generated by institutions are used to purchase pedagogical materials such as textbooks and laboratory supplies, to supplement staff salaries, or to fund professional growth activities such as postdoctoral study, sabbatical leave, or travel to professional conferences, these additional resources—no matter how minor a share of total spending—can have a perceptible impact on education quality.

A critical feature of any policy to encourage funding diversification is to allow incremental resources to remain available in significant measure for use in the institutions which mobilize them. Policies that seek to expropriate resources obtained by the efforts of individual institutions for use by a central authority are self-defeating because they destroy the institutions' incentive to look for savings or generate income.

Financial Support for Needy Students

Little information is available on the capacity of students to pay for university education in systems where tuition and fees are absent or set at token levels. In countries with a large network of private higher education institutions, such as Brazil and the Philippines, there is clear evidence that middle-class families are willing and able to pay the full cost of higher education at private institutions, including at expensive, high-quality institutions. The large number of privately sponsored students from developing countries that attend universities in industrial countries is another indication of that willingness. A recent World Bank study of Latin American countries has estimated that, given the prevailing pattern of income level and distribution in these countries, it would be reasonable to expect students (and their parents) on average to contribute 25 to 30 percent of the per-student cost of public higher education.

At the same time, this study and a recent study on Indonesia have shown that poorer households, or those with more than one family member enrolled in higher education, may not be able to afford university fees. Clearly, cost-sharing cannot be implemented equitably without a functioning student loan program to make funds available to all students who wish to borrow for their education and without scholarship programs that guarantee necessary finan-

cial support to academically qualified poor students unable to absorb the
direct and indirect (forgone earnings) costs of higher education.

Fixed Repayment Loan Schemes

To assist students in meeting the costs of higher education, many countries
have introduced loan schemes, covering tuition or student living expenses, or
both, which are repaid from subsequent earnings after graduation. Experience
to date with existing loan schemes in some fifty industrial and developing
countries, more than half of them in Latin America and the Caribbean, has
been disappointing. Because of heavily subsidized interest rates, high default
rates, and high administrative costs, the repayment proportion of loans (the
"loan recovery ratio") has not been very significant (see table 3.1). In some
cases, the financial performance of loan schemes has been so unsatisfactory
that it would have been cheaper to substitute loans with outright grants. Even
those loan schemes that have functioned reasonably well are quite small in
scale (covering less than 10 percent of the student population), and it is
unclear whether efficient administration could be maintained if the programs
were expanded substantially.

Improving the efficiency and broadening the coverage of existing student
loan programs are major challenges for developing-country governments (see
box 3.1). Despite the poor performance of many loan programs, the experience of Colombia and the Canadian province of Quebec, for example, shows
that it is possible to design and administer financially sustainable programs.
Sustainable loan programs require an effective collection agency, with incentives to minimize evasion and default. Interest rates must be raised to levels
that are positive in real terms if loan programs are to be financially sustainable. An alternative approach to the programming of loan repayments consists
of designing scheduled repayments so that initial payments are smaller than
later ones to approximate the trend in expected income. Such graduated repayment plans can minimize the burden on graduates and improve loan recovery rates.

Income-Contingent Loans

A growing number of countries are adopting income-contingent loan systems,
in which loan repayments are fixed proportions of a graduate's annual income. Although experience to date is limited, such systems achieve a better
balance between effective cost recovery and risk to the borrower. Administration is generally simpler and cheaper under such schemes because loan recovery is handled through existing collection mechanisms, such as the income tax

TABLE 3.1 HIDDEN SUBSIDIES AND GOVERNMENT LOSSES ON SELECTED STUDENT LOAN PROGRAMS

| | Average loan recovery ratio (percentage of loan) | | |
| | Excluding default | Including default | |
Country or province	and administrative cost	and administrative cost	Year
Mortgage loans			
Brazil I	19	2	1983
Venezuela	77	8	1991
Kenya	30	8	1989
Jamaica I	26	8	1987
Colombia I	27	13	1978
Chile	52	18	1989
Honduras	49	27	1991
Indonesia	43	29	1985
Brazil II	38	29	1989
Sweden I	39	30	1988
Jamaica II	44	30	1988
Denmark	48	38	1986
Japan	50	40	1987
United States	71	47	1986
Finland	65	48	1986
Norway	67	52	1986
Colombia II	71	53	1985
Hong Kong	57	53	1985
United Kingdom	74	59	1989
Quebec, Canada	69	63	1989
Barbados	87	67	1988
Income-contingent loans			
Australia	52	43	1990
Sweden II	72	67	1990

Note: Some countries have more than one program. "I" and "II" refer to these.
Source: Albrecht and Ziderman 1992a.

service or the social security system. Income-contingent loans are also more equitable and satisfy more fully the ability-to-pay principle, since graduates' payments are in proportion to their income. For example, the new student support scheme in Sweden minimizes the risk of student default by limiting repayments to 4 percent of income after graduation. Ghana has adopted a similar new student loan program which will collect payments through the social security system. In Australia, income-related loan payments are made

The Stafford Loan Program has been the principal federal government mechanism for promoting access to higher education in the United States. Under the program, all post-secondary students who meet financial need criteria and are enrolled in accredited institutions have access to government-subsidized loans from private commercial banks. Loans can be used at public or private institutions, including vocationally oriented proprietary institutions. The federal government acts as the loan guarantor and pays a direct administration fee to the financial institutions handling the loans.

Since its inception in 1964, the U.S. student loan program has helped millions of students from middle- and low-income families to attend college or to attend higher-quality institutions than they would otherwise have been able to afford. It has allowed the United States to achieve high participation rates in higher education at a much lower cost to government than if that education were provided free to all students. Nonetheless, decisions in the 1970s to try to increase further the access of low-income students to higher education by making subsidized loans available for study at vocationally oriented proprietary institutions, in addition to traditional colleges and universities, have made for an increasingly costly program. During the 1980s, approximately 17 percent of borrowing students failed to repay their debts, resulting in a $3 billion annual government loss. The growing problem of default appears to stem from the high risk involved in guaranteeing loans to all students, without attempting to screen for the quality of the students who receive support or the institutions they plan

through the income tax system. The rate of repayment is 2, 3, or 4 percent of taxable income, depending on how much a graduate earns. The existence of a comprehensive student loan system has enabled Australia to introduce cost-sharing in public higher education and achieve a 30 percent expansion in enrollments during the past five years without a significant increase in public subsidies.

Income-contingent loans offer considerable promise. However, their feasibility depends heavily on the existence of a reliable income taxation system or social security system with access to accurate information about individuals' income and with the administrative capacity to handle loan collection.

Grants and Work-Study Schemes

Government involvement in student loan programs can help ensure that loans are available to academically qualified low-income students. But, in addition

to attend. For example, subsidized loans are available for study even at institutions that do not require students to have a secondary school diploma. Default is by far the highest in proprietary and two-year institutions. In 1989, the rate was 33 percent among students at proprietary schools but only 7 percent among students attending four-year institutions. The experience of the federal student loan scheme in the United States indicates the important benefits that student loan programs offer at the same time as it indicates some of the inherent risks of such lending and, particularly, the way risks can increase as program coverage is extended to a broader and more diverse pool of beneficiaries.

The Colombian Institute of Educational Credit and Training Abroad (ICETEX) student loan program gave its first student loan in 1952 and provides loans to help students from low-income groups attend higher education institutions, both public and private, abroad as well as in Colombia. An important feature of ICETEX is its decentralized structure. There are twenty-one regional offices, each of which manages its own portfolio, appoints its own staff, allocates its own budget, and develops a regional student loan trust fund. ICETEX has been successful in expanding equity and access while maintaining efficiency. Loans are made based on academic merit, financial need, and skill shortage. Geographic representation is also considered. In its forty years of operation, ICETEX has financed more than 400,000 student loans. In 1990, its loan arrears were just 12 percent. While the program is clearly successful, currently only 6 percent of all students enrolled in higher education receive ICETEX loans. An effort is under way to broaden coverage of the program.

Source: Albrecht and Ziderman 1992a.

to the direct tuition costs of higher education, low-income students often have difficulty financing their living expenses while studying, and loan support may not be available for these costs. These students face a further disadvantage in pursuing higher education—forgone earnings, which may be an important source of income for their families. In order to protect equity, governments need to provide support to ensure that poor but able students can pursue higher education. When the University of the Philippines raised tuition fees in the late 1980s, for example, it also provided a special fund to support qualified students from low-income families. Chilean universities also offer grant assistance to academically qualified poor students. Student work-study programs are another vehicle for such assistance. These programs have an administrative advantage over the provision of grants (which requires full financial disclosure from students' families) in that they tend to be self-targeting (that is, students who can afford it prefer not to work while in school).

General Principles for the Design of Student Financial Assistance Programs

Government-subsidized financial assistance programs for academically quali-fied yet financially needy students are an essential complement to cost-shar-ing in higher education. Cost-sharing coupled with student financial assistance is an efficient strategy for achieving expanded coverage and better quality in higher education with a given amount of government resources while protect-ing equity of access. Financial assistance programs that include grant, work-study, and loan programs (whether fixed repayment or income-contingent) allow flexibility in constructing an appropriate overall financial assistance package for each needy student. However, given that in every developing country students attending higher education represent an elite group with income-earning potential significantly higher than that of their peers, it is appropriate that the major form of student financial assistance offered be government-guaranteed student loans rather than grants.

How financial programs are administered is important. Student financial assistance programs which are administered by a central agency *and* that allow students to take their financial assistance package to any institution of their choosing have an important advantage over programs linked to particu-lar institutions: such "student-based" or "portable" financial assistance stimu-lates the competition among educational institutions to offer courses in line with student demand. They establish a situation in which public subsidies increase the educational purchasing power of poor students and put them into exactly the same situation as those paying for their higher education from their own or family funds. The best possible market signals are therefore given to educational institutions. Under such systems, the state does not act as a decisionmaker among institutions, but provides funds to enable poor students to make the same choices as those with more financial resources. In this way, governments can use market forces to stimulate increases in the quality of higher education.

Efficient Resource Allocation and Utilization

Since government funds are likely to remain a large, if not the major source of financing for public higher education, it is important that the allocation of these resources be transparent, rational, and efficient. The criteria used by governments in allocating funding to universities and other institutions should create incentives for these institutions to use scarce funds efficiently. The mechanisms through which transfers are made strongly influence the way in which public funds are used.

Negotiated Budgets

In most countries, the distribution of public resources to tertiary institutions is based on negotiated budgets. This process generally fails to provide incentives for efficient operation and makes it difficult to adjust the distribution of financial resources to changing circumstances (see table 3.2). In the absence of any agreed criteria or information related to the performance of different institutions, government agencies have no politically defensible basis for shifting budgetary allocations. Annual budget decisions tend to reflect historical trends and ensure "political equity" (guaranteeing each institution its traditional share of the total) rather than quality or efficiency. If overall funding is reduced, the tendency of most governments is to adopt across-the-board cuts rather than to evaluate in which institutions and programs cuts are most justified.

TABLE 3.2 SYSTEMS FOR DIRECTLY ALLOCATING RESOURCES TO INSTITUTIONS OF HIGHER EDUCATION, SELECTED COUNTRIES

Negotiated	Input-based	Output-based	Quality-based
Algeria	Canada	Denmark	Chile
Argentina	China	Finland	
Brazil	France	Israel	
Ghana	Hungary	Netherlands	
Greece	Indonesia	Australia	
Guinea	Japan		
Honduras	Nigeria		
India	Norway		
Italy	South Africa		
Jordan	Sweden		
Kenya	United Kingdom		
Morocco	Viet Nam		
Nepal			
Niger			
Pakistan			
Peru			
Philippines			
Sudan			
Tanzania			
Venezuela			
Yemen			

Source: Albrecht and Ziderman 1992c.

Alternative Allocation Mechanisms

Alternative mechanisms which link funding to performance criteria are being used increasingly by OECD countries and could be considered by developing countries as well. Such mechanisms can create powerful incentives for more efficient use of resources. The models most commonly used link funding either to "inputs" (the numbers of students enrolled, adjusted by program) or "outputs" (the numbers of graduates). Only one country to date (Chile) has attempted to link funding explicitly to qualitative, rather than quantitative, indicators of institutional performance.

Input-based funding. In a number of countries, tertiary institutions receive their budgets calculated on the basis of a funding formula that combines enrollment figures and unit costs and uses coefficients or weights to provide incentives for internal distribution of resources. The most common formulas differentiate institutions on the basis of the numbers of students enrolled in different fields of study, levels of education (undergraduate, post-graduate, doctoral, and so on), certain facts about the type of institution (including location, size, and mission within the system), and the socioeconomic levels and academic quality of students. The weights thus reflect the differential costs faced by different institutions—for example, for engineering students compared with art students. By using such weights, governments can also exercise indirect influence over the distribution of student intake.

A major issue with input-based funding is how it relates to admissions policy. If the government does not take an active role in determining the level and distribution of student intake, then its budgetary commitment is theoretically open-ended: it must either increase the higher education budget or reduce its payment per student when resources are scarce. One way of resolving this problem is to set a price the government will pay per student, but only for a fixed number of students. Additional students can be admitted by institutions on a fee-for-service basis. Such an approach was adopted by Viet Nam in 1989 and is currently being considered in Uganda.

Many input-based funding mechanisms fail to provide sufficient incentives for efficiency. When input-based funding essentially compensates institutions for costs incurred, it often does not create incentives for institutions to improve the quality of their programs or to lower costs. However, governments can establish cost norms in their input-based funding formulas and link these to norms relating to the length of study for particular programs to create incentives for increased efficiency.

Output-based funding. Output-based funding mechanisms most commonly allocate government financing to institutions on the basis of their effectiveness in producing graduates (see box 3.2). Such an approach can reduce student failure and repetition, which may result from poor selection and poor preparation in the course selected as well overgenerous programs of student support. In countries such as Australia, Denmark, and the Netherlands, the introduction of output-based funding formulas has been associated with reductions in student wastage and improvement in the overall efficiency of the public higher education system and the efficiency of public resource use. One of the challenges of output-based funding is to provide incentives that will improve performance without creating excessive disruption to teaching or research activities if the distribution of enrollment and funding allocations shift. Another difficulty associated with output-based funding is that it emphasizes the number of graduates rather than the quality that training institutions provide.

Quality-based funding. Among the sweeping reforms of the higher education system adopted by Chile in the early 1980s was a new funding mechanism to allocate a significant share of government support for higher education to institutions on the basis of their quality. As a proxy for quality, the Indirect Funding Program (Apoyo Fiscal Indirecto, or AFI) looks at where the top-ranked students entering higher education each year choose to study. Institutions receive a financial award from the government for each entering student who scored among the top 27,500 in the university aptitude test administered annually to all high school graduates. The AFI awards range in value, depending on how high the individual's test score was. The highest value awards represent a significant share of the total cost of one year of study at a typical

---

BOX 3.2 OUTPUT-BASED FUNDING IN THE NETHERLANDS AND DENMARK

The Netherlands' new funding formula provides more budgetary support for students who complete their degree programs in the time expected. The normal length of a course is 4 years. The formula grants a university 4.5 years of annual unit cost funding per graduate, but only 1.5 years for students who have not completed their programs in the normal length of time.

Denmark has used a somewhat similar approach since the early 1980s. The government provides funding to universities based on the number of students who successfully complete their annual examinations, penalizes institutions with high failure rates, and encouraging universities to weed out poorly performing students and raise entry requirements. At the same time, the government has reduced the tenure of student scholarships and based renewal on academic performance.

Source: Albrecht and Ziderman 1992c.

institution. All higher education institutions, whether public or private, and whether full-university or two-year institute, are eligible to receive this support. The objective of the AFI program is to stimulate competition among institutions to improve their quality and thus to attract the best students. Although it appears that the program has indeed created incentives in this direction, Chilean researchers have observed that the lack of objective information about the academic quality of different institutions undermines the ability of entering students to make sound choices. The impact of the program could be strengthened with complementary actions by the government to make standardized information and evaluations of different institutions' programs publicly available.

To be effective, funding formulas of all types that support the core budgets of public institutions must be transparent, encourage flexibility, and take into account the normative costs of different levels and programs of study, with enrollment changes indexed to avoid wide fluctuations in per student funding. In addition, formulas can encourage internal efficiency either by relating allocations for students to the normal length of time needed to complete a degree or through funding the number of graduates. Reliance on such funding mechanisms will bring about a better use of available resources by increasing internal efficiency and encouraging institutions to reduce noninstructional expenses and focus on training and research.

CHAPTER FOUR

Redefining the Role of Government

THE TRADITIONALLY strong role of the state in higher education has its origins in political and economic circumstances—elite systems,
guaranteed public sector employment, and stable economies—that have radi-
cally changed. The types of reforms discussed above imply profound changes
in the relationship between government and higher education. For most countries, they also imply considerable expansion of the private sector in higher
education. Nonetheless, there are two important economic justifications for
government support of higher education:

■ Higher education investments generate external benefits important for economic development, such as the long-term returns from basic research and
from technology development and transfer; because these benefits cannot be
captured by individuals, private investment alone in higher education would
be socially suboptimal.

■ Imperfections in capital markets (related to the lack of collateral for education investments) constrain the ability of individuals to borrow adequately for
education. This undermines, in particular, the participation of meritorious but
economically disadvantaged groups in higher education.

An important point to note regarding research is that the joint-product
nature of modern universities (that is, complementarity between teaching and

research, and between undergraduate and graduate programs) and the high degree of cross-subsidization across disciplines and levels of studies make it difficult to look at the "research" components of higher education institutions in isolation from other activities.

In most developing countries, however, the extent of government involvement in higher education has far exceeded what is economically efficient. The crisis of higher education, particularly in the public sector, is stimulating a change in the extent, objectives, and modalities of government intervention in higher education in order to ensure a more efficient use of public resources. Rather than direct controls, the government's responsibility is becoming that of providing an enabling policy environment for both public and private higher education institutions and of using the leverage of public funding to stimulate these institutions to meet national training and research needs. Successful implementation of higher education reforms has been shown to depend on a mode of governance that emphasizes:

- A coherent policy framework
- Reliance on incentives and market-oriented instruments to implement policies
- Increased management autonomy for public institutions.

Establishing a Coherent Policy Framework

In establishing a coherent framework for higher education, both government policies and effective structures for government oversight are necessary.

The Role of Government Policies

Higher education *systems* are a relatively new phenomenon, representing the outcome of successive, often unarticulated, government and private initiatives over a long period of time. Many countries have witnessed the proliferation of post-secondary education institutions operating under various ministries without much effort to rationalize the use of public resources. Responsibility for different types of higher education is often fragmented among government departments. National research priorities and funding may be determined by bodies that have no responsibility for higher education and human resource development. The training activities of private higher education institutions may not be subject to any government supervision at all. Oversight of the system and its linkages to primary and secondary education and to other economic sectors is often lacking. Even in the former socialist republics of Central and Eastern Europe, where economic life was dominated by central planning, the higher education sector was characterized by administrative fragmentation.

Whether public or private, universities and colleges, polytechnics, technical and training institutions, and other higher education institutions all have different but related training functions. Guiding the development of a differentiated higher education system requires a well-defined legal framework and consistent policies. This in turn requires a long-term vision on the part of policymakers for the sector as a whole and for the role of each type of institution, public and private, within that whole (see box 4.1).

The recent experience of Hungary is a notable example of effective government policies to guide the development of the higher education system and the introduction of necessary reforms. The disintegration of the socialist regime has had profound implications for the country's higher education facilities. Faced with problems of inadequate quality, underfunding, and low levels of tertiary enrollment in comparison with OECD countries, the Hungarian

---

BOX 4.1 SETTING THE POLICY FRAMEWORK FOR HIGHER EDUCATION IN CALIFORNIA

California pioneered the establishment of a policy framework for a state system of higher education in the United States when it developed and implemented its first Master Plan in 1959–60. The primary issues considered at that time were the future roles of the public and private sectors and, in particular, how the public sector should be governed and coordinated to avoid duplication and waste. Major principles that emerged from the initial master plan still shape the state's system today:

■ Recognition of different missions for the four components of the higher education system (University of California, California State University, community colleges, and private universities and junior colleges)

■ Establishment of a statutory coordinating body for the entire system

■ Differential admission pools for the University and State Colleges

■ Eligibility of students attending private institutions for the state scholarship program.

The California Master Plan for Higher Education, which is revised about every ten years, is not a rigid blueprint to control centrally the development of California's system of higher education. Rather, it sets some general parameters, focuses primarily on the boundaries among the four sectors of higher education, and strives for a system that balances equity, quality, and efficiency.

Sources: OECD 1990; Clark 1990.

---

authorities initiated, in collaboration with the World Bank, a medium-term reform and development program. After a detailed review of the present state of the higher education system and an assessment of the need for comprehensive reform, the decision was made to prepare a new, unified legal framework that encompasses the entire higher education system, including the Academy of Sciences, the universities, and the non-university institutions. The proposed law defines a new regulatory environment for institutions and a new division of responsibilities and duties among the state, the public universities, and new private universities. It reflects a move away from the traditional system of state control toward a more competitive system with increased institutional autonomy and a normative financing system for public resources. The law seeks to establish a decentralized financing, budgeting, and ownership system and provides criteria for the recognition and operation of different types of institutions (see box 6.3 below).

The policy framework for higher education needs to be linked to specific national conditions. For instance, civil service salary scales, employment and labor market policies, and the national science and technology investment framework all have a decisive impact on the performance and evolution of higher education institutions, as does the relationship between them and the primary and secondary subsectors.

Planning higher education development is not a mechanistic and dirigist exercise to impose quantitative targets at the central level. It is a systemic management activity to guide long-term development, assess risks and constraints, and seek alternative ways to ensure long-term viability and improve quality. Such an exercise focuses on economic growth and technological development strategies, the contribution of higher education to bolster these strategies, the overall demand for graduates, the cost and benefits of various forms of training, and the distribution of costs in the education sector.

Finally, recent experience shows that successful reform depends on decisionmakers building consensus among the various constituents of the higher education subsector. In many countries universities have a long tradition of political dissent and active participation in the political process. In these situations students are not passive objects of reform but key political actors whose vocal demands are difficult to ignore. In some of the former socialist republics of Eastern and Central Europe, resistance to reform has come from technical ministries or departments reluctant to relinquish control over the institutions that formerly operated under their exclusive authority.

A potentially effective approach consists of initiating, under the umbrella of an official steering committee, a national consultation on the need for and the content of reform. Involving all of the sectors concerned, including university administrators, faculty, students, ministry officials, and employers, the steering committee and its working groups greatly increase the chances of achieving a consensus. Endeavors along these lines are under way at present in several African countries, including Cameroon, Ghana, and Senegal.

Effective Structures for Government Policy and Oversight

Many countries lack effective institutions for establishing the policy framework for higher education, guiding budgetary allocations, evaluating institutions' performance, and publishing this information for the benefit of prospective students.

Some governments have established national councils and other bodies to advise on higher education policies. In Ghana, for example, the government recently embarked on an exhaustive reappraisal of the role and mission of higher education and launched reforms to rationalize the network of institutions, improve the quality of teaching, and secure the financial viability of the system. A National Implementation Committee was set up to initiate reforms and coordinate their execution. A National Council on Higher Education has just been set up in Uganda to strengthen planning. The National Council is designed to operate as a consultative body, working in close collaboration with an inter-ministerial Capacity Building Secretariat that prepares plans for human resource development. Members will be drawn from universities and colleges, government ministries, and public and private enterprises. Its functions will be to project enrollments, costs, and financial requirements; advise external aid and lending agencies on investment needs; register and accredit institutions; sanction new programs; coordinate admission policies for diploma-granting institutions; and prepare a strategy for reforming the financing and management of public higher education. In addition to these national initiatives, African countries also benefit from a regional process of mutual exchange and support for higher education policymaking (see box 4.2).

While the organization of policy advisory bodies that have responsibility for higher education varies, such bodies share three common characteristics when they are effective. First, they are either quasi-governmental or fully autonomous; that is, they are in practice independent of government. Second, they have representation from various components of the subsector and from outside the higher education system. Third, their responsibilities involve assessing priorities for both enrollment growth and future investment.

Relying on Incentive Instruments to Implement Policies

Through subsidizing higher studies and university research, governments can affect the supply of graduates to the labor market and give direction to gradu-

BOX 4.2 REGIONAL POLICY SUPPORT IN AFRICA

The Working Group on Higher Education (WGHE) is one of several Working Groups established by the Donors to African Education (DAE) in 1989 as a mechanism to further collaboration between multi- and bilateral development agencies and African governments and institutions. With a membership of fifteen aid and lending agencies, the WGHE seeks to improve the effectiveness of development assistance to African universities. A roughly equal but rotating number of African university leaders, scholars, and government officials are invited to participate in the semi-annual WGHE meetings, which have been held in Ghana, Kenya, Mozambique, Senegal, and Tanzania. Coordination responsibilities for the WGHE rest with the World Bank.

The meetings have progressively explored issues of university finance, governance, management, graduate programs, women's participation, staff retention, and higher education policies. Studies on these topics commissioned for the WGHE include *Universities in Africa: Strategies for Stabilization and Revitalization* (Saint 1992), and *Financial Diversification and Income Generation at Selected African Universities* (Blair 1991). The papers and meetings have helped African universities and representatives from aid and lending agencies to improve

ate training and research. Where circumstances require correction of labor market and enrollment distortions, governments do best to rely on direct incentives to students, such as scholarships and student loans, and on resource allocation processes rather than issuing directives to control the size and distribution of student intake. Any significant shift in the size or composition of enrollments has implications that governments need to anticipate and provide for in the long term, including the need for qualified academic staff and instructional and research facilities.

In many countries governments have a strong role in determining the level and composition of enrollments, reflecting a time when the public sector was able to absorb most of the products of the higher education system and when the state financed most or all higher education costs. Enrollments are still all too often determined by fixed-coefficient labor requirements forecasting. Experience has shown that this type of labor power planning does not anticipate the impact of technological change on the demand for skills or take account of the incentives that labor markets provide for employers to adjust the demand for skilled labor. The large errors associated with labor power forecasts tend to increase with the length of the forecasting period.

The level and distribution of student intake should normally reflect existing rather than anticipated or past employment opportunities. Governments

their understanding of each other's interests and constraints, generating consensus on the need for locally managed strategic approaches.

As a result of this collaboration, the relationship between universities and aid and lending agencies is now being cast in a broader institutional development context as opposed to the prevailing project orientation. Universities in Mozambique and Tanzania, for example, have carried out institutional self-assessments and used them to produce development plans. Others have begun this process. Aid and lending agencies are being asked to flexibly support the major elements of these plans, according universities greater autonomy in funding management in return for improved accountability in the use of their resources. The WGHE also suggests institutional twinning arrangements as a useful means of shoring up weak disciplinary areas, accessing international scientific knowledge, and transferring needed management techniques. It advocates the standardization of reporting systems to aid and lending agencies so as to reduce administrative burdens on universities. During the past year, several agencies that belong to the WGHE have announced policy changes that will bring their funding practices more in line with these recommendations.

---

should not interfere with market mechanisms or with institutional priorities unless the need for state intervention is compelling and economically justified. An example could be public subsidies for some specialties in the applied sciences with high private costs and/or low private returns but high social return.

Governments can help higher education institutions strengthen the quality of education in many ways. For example, they can assist institutions in selecting students by organizing and improving admission examinations. This is particularly important where academic secondary education is highly variable in quality and where requirements for graduation have little relationship to the knowledge, skills, and levels of mastery required for entry. Governments can help establish minimum standards of admission to the various types of public institutions and raise these in order to improve the quality and reduce the variability of secondary education. For instance, countries that have adopted the British system of education (for example, Ghana, Hong Kong, Kenya, Singapore, and Uganda) and a number of East Asian countries (for example, China and Korea) have used nationwide university entrance examinations to select students. At the same time, such examinations set national standards for secondary education. China particularly stands out as an example. After ten years of neglect of higher education during the Cultural Revolution, China reintroduced a nationwide university entrance examination in 1977 in order to galvanize secondary school teachers and students to pay attention to academic study and to have a consistent criterion for selection for admission to higher education.

For students to make rational choices, they need good information on the costs and quality of courses at different institutions and on the labor market opportunities for graduates of different courses. Governments can help strengthen the quality of education by ensuring that such information is widely available (for example, on institutions' costs, relative performance, and on salaries in the labor market) and by certifying quality through accreditation.

Governments can either accredit institutions and establish procedures for recognizing degrees, diplomas, and certificates themselves, or allow private accrediting agencies and professional associations to perform this function. In matters relating to examinations, accreditation, and recognition, the role of the government should be reconciled with the size and characteristics of the system as well as with its capacity to finance higher education and employ graduates. In small, relatively undifferentiated, mainly public higher education systems and in countries where most employment growth occurs in the public sector, governments have a stronger role in these matters. As higher

---

BOX 4.3 STATE CONTROL VERSUS STATE SUPERVISION

There are two broad governance models that governments can adopt in managing their systems of higher education. The first is the *state-control model*, in which the system has been created by and is entirely funded and regulated by the state. The higher education system of Cameroon illustrates how the state-control model operates in many francophone African countries. The Higher Education and Research Ministry is the regulatory body for higher education, the minister holding administrative and political authority over all institutions. The chancellors are presidential appointees, and all academic appointments must be sanctioned by the government. Institutions do not select their students; anyone who successfully completes secondary school and earns a baccalauréat is eligible for admission. The budget for all institutions, which is not tied to any evaluation mechanism, is determined and allocated by the state and is highly skewed in favor of student support. This has led in recent years to decreased investments in institutional infrastructure and learning materials and to a marked decline in the quality of instruction.

At the other end of the continuum lies Chile, which since the higher education reform of the early 1980s has followed the *state supervision model*. Chilean institutions are now

---

education systems increase in size and complexity, responsibilities for quality assurance are best devolved onto institutional or professional organizations that operate independently of government. Most government regulatory powers should be delegated, apart from those pertaining to the legal establishment of institutions and the standardization of academic credentials.

Increasing the Autonomy and Accountability of Public Institutions

Greater institutional autonomy is the key to the successful reform of public higher education, especially reform aimed at resource diversification and more efficient use of resources. Recent experience shows that autonomous institutions are more responsive to incentives for quality improvements and efficiency gains. In France, Japan, and the Netherlands, the government has granted increased financial autonomy to individual faculties and departments in national universities to stimulate innovation in research and teaching. In Chile, Thailand, and Viet Nam, in order to redistribute the costs of higher education, the government has transferred many powers and responsibilities affecting costs to institutions, while establishing policy structures to guide the development of the system from a greater distance (see box 4.3).

---

largely demand-driven. Public institutions and private universities alike make their decisions independently. Public institutions are loosely coordinated through the Rectors' Council, an autonomous body chaired by the minister of education. Private institutions have no relationship with the government unless they have chosen to participate in the voluntary accreditation process overseen by the Higher Council of Education to encourage quality improvement efforts in the private subsector. Only public institutions receive a direct budgetary allocation from the government, whereas private institutions finance their budget through tuition and fees. Both types of institutions are expected to generate complementary income through fees for services, research contracts, and other projects. Institutions are free to determine how their budgets should be spent. The government sponsors a merit scholarship scheme for students attending either public or private institutions. As a result of the reform of Chilean higher education, the system has become more differentiated. The total number of institutions increased from 8 to 310, opportunities for access have grown as institutions became regionally dispersed, and the provision of higher education is dominated by self-sustaining private institutions.

Sources: van Vught 1991; Ngu, Ngu, and Atangana 1992; Brunner 1992.

If income diversification is to be pursued effectively, institutions must have an incentive to generate and use a financial surplus. They must be allowed to keep the additional resources they raise to finance quality improvements instead of being compelled, as in Uganda and many countries, to transfer them to the treasury. In some countries, Brazil for example, several universities are prevented by law from imposing tuition, and in Indonesia and elsewhere tuition fees are set only with government approval. Such restrictions create management rigidities and inefficiencies. Conversely, a diversified resource base is the best guarantee of institutional autonomy. Autonomy remains largely an empty concept as long as institutions are dependent on a single government funding source.

Decentralization of all key management functions to higher education institutions themselves is a sine qua non for successful reform, especially with respect to funding diversification and more efficient use of resources. Higher education institutions must be in a position to exercise meaningful control over the principal factors affecting their costs. Each institution should be able to set admissions requirements, assess tuition and fees, and establish eligibility criteria for financial assistance to needy students, in order to ensure that the number and distribution of new students is at a level compatible with its resources. Institutions should also have the power to recruit and retrench personnel, which represents the major cost factor for most higher education institutions. This flexibility is essential if universities are to be able to build up new programs in response to new labor market demands and to control costs by eliminating faculty when student-teacher ratios in other departments decline below efficient levels. Salary scales should be set independently across institutions, so that these may attract faculty of the caliber desired.

Public funding can also be transferred in ways which support institutional autonomy. Once agreement is reached with the government regarding the annual budgetary allocation, for example, institutions should be guaranteed access to these resources when needed. Effective management also means that institutions must have the ability to reallocate resources internally, which in many countries is denied by a rigid line-item budget system. To encourage institutional planning, operating funds should be received in the form of block grants or be subject to few restrictions on the transfer of funds from one expenditure to another. Institutions require this flexibility to cross-subsidize programs, launch new initiatives, and provide resources to academic units to strengthen their programs. In Hong Kong, for example, universities, polytechnics, and colleges receive block grants from the University and Polytechnic Grants Committee, and they are subject to very few restrictions on how they use these funds.

Along with increased autonomy, higher education institutions need to be held accountable for their performance. This involves monitoring the quality of their training and research outputs, the relevance of their programs, and their use of public subsidies. It also requires more sophisticated evaluation capacity than most governments have in place today. Countries that rely on performance-based allocation mechanisms are in a better position to foster efficient use of public resources. Performance indicators are most effective when they are clearly related to institutional goals and when they are used as aids in decisionmaking, not as rigid determinants of funding.

Autonomy and accountability also have implications for the governance structure and management culture of institutions. An independent governance structure could include an assembly consisting of members of the university community, a lay governing board with broad representation from the wider community, and a vice chancellor or rector with proven management skills appointed by the board on the advice of the assembly.

Many higher education institutions need stronger management to administer their resources. Even within the limits of existing financial resources, much progress can be achieved if strict management procedures and simplified budgetary rules are followed. Improving management practices also involves the development and utilization of comprehensive management information systems to support the decisionmaking process. Reliable data on enrollments, internal efficiency, expenditures, and costs are still not available in many institutions. Sound management information is essential for planning activities, allocating resources, making management decisions, and guiding innovations. The introduction of computerized management information systems in countries such as Australia, Malaysia, and New Zealand has helped public higher education institutions improve their efficiency.

CHAPTER FIVE

Focusing on Quality, Responsiveness, and Equity

In THE context of a revised policy framework that allows more diversity in the provision of higher education and greater financial sustainability of institutions, the main elements of a strategy to improve the performance of higher education, against which progress can be measured, are:

- Improved quality of teaching and research
- Increased responsiveness of higher education to labor market demands
- Greater equity.

Enhancing the Quality of Training and Research

To produce well-trained graduates and significant research outputs, higher education institutions must be able to bring together the minimal inputs necessary for successful performance: well-prepared secondary school graduates, competent and motivated faculty, and facilities with essential instructional and research equipment and materials. Effective institutions are also open to international exchanges and rely on sound evaluation mechanisms for assessing and improving the quality of teaching and research.

Well-Prepared Students

Effective selection is important because the quality of students admitted into an institution affects the quality and internal efficiency of training. To educate their students effectively, institutions should be able to enroll only as many applicants as they can responsibly teach, and to accept only students who possess the knowledge and ability to benefit fully from their studies. Selectivity should help ensure that enrollment growth is related to instructional capacity and, if selection criteria have good predictive validity, that opportunities for further studies will be allocated to those who are most likely to benefit academically. Students perform best when they follow courses of study that match their abilities and interests. Yet in many countries institutions have little influence on the selection, intake, and distribution of enrollment, which is the responsibility of government. Expressed preferences often have little influence on the course of study to which students are admitted. The often dramatically negative impact on the quality of instruction and on student motivation of such a policy is most visible in countries in which graduation from academic secondary education automatically confers a right to publicly financed higher education.

To increase selection efficiency, high standards of performance in academic subjects must be set for secondary school graduates seeking admission. This result can be achieved either through a national examination—as is done in China, Thailand, and in India for admission to the Indian Institutes of Technology—or by allowing institutions or departments to establish their own admission criteria, such as a combination of entrance examination scores, high school grades, and an aptitude test, in conformity with minimum standards established by accrediting bodies. This type of selection mechanism encourages each institution to define its niche in the overall higher education structure and select its students accordingly.

High-quality academic secondary education is the only secure foundation for high-quality higher education. Strengthening science education and foreign language training is of special importance. In universities and many other higher education institutions in developing countries, the medium of instruction is often a foreign language. Where an indigenous language is used, foreign language training at the secondary level is even more important, since it increases access to information used for instruction at higher levels.

Qualified Teaching Staff

A highly competent and motivated teaching staff and a supportive professional culture are essential in building excellence. Staff numbers, qualifications, deployment, and remuneration are central in determining the quality of instruction. Even though formal staff qualifications (the proportion of staff with Ph.D. or master's degrees) may be seen as the best single indicator of

institutional quality, the relationship between the quality of training and research depends on the mission of the institution. Only in research universities
or in fast-changing fields may it be appropriate to require Ph.D.s of all senior
faculty and to base promotion primarily on research performance. In other
institutions, more emphasis should be given to teaching, supervisory, administrative, and service abilities when recruiting and promoting staff.

Public university salaries in many countries are linked to civil service pay
scales, which are often low in comparison with private sector employment and
which reward seniority rather than merit. Promotion based on seniority rather
than performance also often discourages graduates from entering academic
life. Where salaries are insufficient, faculty members are likely to take up
other jobs at the expense of their academic commitments. In Ghana, for
example, universities had to establish a supplement equal to 50 percent of the
base salary in order to counter a "brain drain" caused by the economic crisis of
the 1980s. There must be nonpecuniary professional rewards, too, such as
opportunities for professional communication and peer recognition.

Supplying Adequate Pedagogical Inputs

Scientific laboratories and workshops need to be well equipped and supplied
with consumables, and provision must be made for proper maintenance of
buildings and equipment. Upgrading university libraries is also a priority,
provided of course that library use is supported by appropriate methods of
instruction and examination that emphasize independent work. Institutions
should operate with well-stocked and up-to-date libraries that have sufficient
study space and that cater to the teaching and research needs of the various
academic departments. Cost-effective access to current information, for example through CD-ROMs and electronic networks, is also needed for science
research and training.

Stimulating International Exchange

Leading higher education institutions must be open to international influ-
ences. Since the establishment of the first universities in North Africa and
Europe, all great universities have recruited students and staff both locally and
internationally. Africa's oldest and most prestigious universities, such as Dakar,
Ibadan, and Makerere, were founded as regional institutions with an international staff and close ties to leading metropolitan institutions. The newer
centers of excellence in the developing world—the Indian Institutes of Technology and Management, the Korean Advanced Institute of Science and
Technology, the National University of Singapore, and the University of the
Philippines at Los Banyos, for example—have international missions and

policies to promote international contacts. These can include reserved places for foreign students, international advertisement of academic positions, extra-institutional peer review of candidates for promotion, international participation in internal evaluations of academic units, secondment of staff to foreign institutions, partnership with foreign universities, and degree and nondegree programs designed to attract foreign students.

Many developing countries have invested heavily in overseas training for university staff, often with external support. This has been successful in countries such as the Republic of Korea and Indonesia, where most returning graduates have been able to find good employment. In other situations it has led to the loss of educated citizens to other countries. Sometimes graduates returning to their home country are not able to obtain employment in their area of specialization or to continue their research. "Sandwich" advanced degree programs, where the home university defines a relevant research program in cooperation with an overseas institution, are much more likely to contribute to stronger research and training programs at local universities than traditional doctoral programs overseas.

Strengthening Evaluation Mechanisms

Perhaps the most important determinant of academic performance is the ability to evaluate and monitor the quality of training and research outputs. Recent studies indicate that, in order to evaluate the quality of teaching, self-evaluation mechanisms can promote a sense of real institutional responsibility. In a number of countries, universities have initiated periodic performance reviews, including the quality and relevance of programs, internal efficiency, and financing needs. To evaluate faculty teaching, the most frequently used methods are reliance on student ratings, evaluation by a department chairperson, evaluation of course outlines, peer evaluation, and teaching awards. What is important is that the procedures and criteria for evaluation be transparent and that the outcome be used to take corrective actions.

Independent assessments to measure output quality can help set and preserve high standards of performance (see box 5.1). The validity of the assessment process can be increased by setting up systems of external accreditation, examination, and evaluation, especially for advanced scientific disciplines. The objective is to establish minimum criteria for the organization and provision of academic programs that discourage ineffective practices and reinforce positive characteristics. Examples include Korea's Ministry of Education, which from the late 1960s began setting standards for the country's public and private universities and colleges. In many countries, professional associations fulfill important coordinating and planning functions to monitor, evaluate, certify, and accredit higher education institutions. This is intended to promote

**BOX   5.1 ACCREDITATION
OF TEACHER TRAINING
INSTITUTIONS**

In Indonesia, the World Bank supported the introduction of accreditation mechanisms in a project to
improve teacher training standards
in public institutions. The experiment
with accreditation has had some success but has necessitated significant
modifications of international accreditation practices. A pilot program was
established in 1987 to develop a
scheme to accredit teacher training
programs in selected institutions, after the government decided to upgrade all pre-service teacher training
institutions to university status. The
objective was to agree upon a set of
standards by which all teacher training institutions could be evaluated as
well as to establish a baseline for institutional development. Five autonomous Institutes of Teacher Training
and Pedagogy were selected on a
competitive basis to participate in the
program, and eleven teaching subject areas were identified. Small
planning grants were made available to each institution to enable
them to do a self study, which was
externally evaluated and validated
by professionals and education
practitioners. Importance was
placed on ensuring that these vali-
dations were nonthreatening and
collegial. Shortcomings, when
found, were viewed not as some-
thing to be penalized. On the contrary, they were perceived as
starting points to initiate necessary
improvements. The pilot study was
useful in generating acceptance for
accreditation as a mechanism to
improve teacher training. An Education Consortium was subse-
quently established to advise the
Directorate General of Higher Education on standards of teacher training and investments in qualitative
improvements.

Source: Eisemon 1992b.

standardization of programs and is useful in ensuring the equivalence of
degrees, diplomas, and certificates awarded. Professional recognition and
accreditation typically involves external assessment of instructional activities
and plans for institutional self-improvement.

As illustrated by the recent experience of Western European countries, the
most effective evaluation mechanisms emphasize self-evaluation on institutional mission and performance combined with external assessment procedures, whether by professional associations or a government oversight agency.

Responding to Changing Economic Demands

Many developing countries, as well as the formerly socialist countries of
Europe and Central Asia, pursue economic growth strategies based on techno-

logical accumulation. In this context it is critically important that training and research programs respond to the evolving demands of the economy. The institutions responsible for advanced training and research programs should be guided by representatives from the productive sectors. The participation of private sector representatives on the governing boards of public and private higher education institutions can help ensure the relevance of academic programs. Financial incentives for joint industry-university cooperative research, corporate-sponsored internships for students, and part-time academic appointments for professionals from the productive sectors can all help strengthen the linkages and communication between the higher education system and other sectors of the economy. In the newly industrialized economies of East Asia, for instance, government-provided funding for cooperative research was a strong incentive for firms and universities to establish linkages.

Strengthening Postgraduate Training and Research

The failure to sustain strong postgraduate programs limits the development impact of higher education. Postgraduate education is important for at least three reasons. First, universities in developing countries are the locus of fundamental as well as applied research. Second, graduates of postgraduate programs are needed to staff private and public research and development (R&D) units and high-technology-based manufacturing activities. This is the most important mechanism through which research results are transferred, thereby changing the technological bases of agricultural and manufacturing production. Finally, postgraduate programs in most countries are important for staff development and thus for improving the quality of higher education in general.

Efforts to strengthen postgraduate education must take account of conditions in the higher education system as a whole. Strong undergraduate programs are necessary to ensure a sufficient pool of students qualified for further study, many of whom may be recruited from institutions that are not involved in postgraduate training and research. Students interested in and eligible for postgraduate studies are usually a relatively small group with multiple career options. It is easier to attract them into postgraduate programs when career opportunities and adequate support through fellowships are available.

Three principles should guide the organization of national research systems. First, it is preferable to combine graduate education and research in the same institutions. This raises the quality of both training and research, which, in most basic sciences, tends to be more efficiently performed in universities than in separate government research institutions. Second, because of the high personnel and facilities costs for postgraduate education and research in experimental sciences, most of the capacity for advanced scientific training and research is best concentrated in a few institutions where programs can be adequately supported. Third, with respect to the institutional division of labor in national research systems, universities have significant comparative advantages in fundamental and interdisciplinary research as a result of their size, training missions, and distribution of resources across many fields of study. Other public and private scientific institutions are more suitable than universities for most applied research.

Adequate working conditions and strong incentives that motivate researchers are necessary to create a supportive environment for quality research. Academic staff must be sufficiently well remunerated to undertake research and related teaching activities on a full-time basis. Strong performance in research and postgraduate education should be rewarded through professional advancement and nonpecuniary professional rewards.

Because of the high costs and normally high governmental and institutional subsidization of postgraduate studies, support for the establishment and improvement of programs must be highly selective. To improve program quality and efficiency, competition among academic units for discretionary resources should be stimulated. The principle of competition should extend to the allocation of funding for staff research, which, in turn, should support a high proportion of the nontuition costs of postgraduate training. Competitive research funding programs can be designed to achieve other purposes as well, for example, to increase the volume of research in fields of high priority for national scientific and industrial policies and to foster interdisciplinary and inter-institutional team research in specialties for which research and training can be strengthened through collaboration. To ensure accountability, reward productivity, and encourage improvement in the quality of research, renewal of research support should be contingent on the publication of results in journals that have high professional visibility locally and internationally. Importance should also be placed on the production of candidates for degree programs supported by staff research projects, especially in countries in which it is necessary to build up the domestic scientific community.

Regional Cooperation

Because they have limited human and financial resources, difficulty in taking advantage of economies of scale, and a modest-size labor market, small and low-income countries face specific constraints on the type and size of higher education programs that they can afford (see box 5.2). The only way of establishing or maintaining cost-effective graduate training and research programs may be to organize them on a regional basis. Each participating country would support a few strong national programs operating as regional centers of specialization within the framework of a multi-state institution such as the University of the South Pacific or the University of the West Indies.

In Africa, where supra-national institutions such as the now defunct University of East Africa have proven difficult to sustain, recent forms of regional cooperation have pursued a more efficient division of labor within a multi-country network of existing national universities. Examples include graduate programs in agriculture under the Special Programme for African Agricultural Research (SPAAR), a collaborative master's program in economics launched by the African Economic Research Consortium (AERC), and graduate training in engineering coordinated through the African Network of Scientific and

---

BOX 5.2 REGIONAL COOPERATION

In providing higher education, small and low-income countries should find an appropriate balance among local institutions, regional institutions, and overseas training. Development of local institutions in small and low-income countries has been significant but uncoordinated. As new education and training needs have emerged in the past twenty years, there has been a tendency to create new post-secondary institutions under separate authority rather than incorporating new functions into existing institutions. The result has been a proliferation of small uneconomical teaching units that to some extent duplicate each other's functions. For example, Fiji, with a population of 700,000, has five public sector higher education institutions: the Fiji Institute of Technology, two teachers colleges, the Fiji School of Medicine, and the College of Agriculture.

In many instances, establishing and operating a full-fledged national university is not economically viable. A logical option would be for each country to analyze its specific needs, constraints, and opportunities, determine the programs and disciplines it requires and can teach best, and take advantage of economies of scale and subject specialization. It should be more feasible in the case of countries such as the Caribbean Islands and the Pacific Island nations, which are affiliated with regional universities like the University of the West Indies (UWI) and the University of the South Pacific (USP). UWI, for instance, has gone a long way toward organizing the teaching of first- and second-year courses in local institutions and focusing on more specialized courses at the regional university. The alternative of sending students overseas should be reserved for specialized postgraduate courses that cannot affordably be offered in the region.

Source: World Bank 1992a.

Technological Institutions (ANSTI). Lessons gleaned from these experiences suggest that a structured process of regular institutional interaction is necessary to build trust, forge consensus, and hold the group accountable for its decisions; that an institutional mechanism is necessary to manage this process; and that external funding is critical for initial success. These experiences suggest that regional cooperation is most likely to be achieved by identifying and strengthening existing national institutions or programs that possess a convincing record of achievement and the potential to operate successfully as multi-country or regional centers. Instead of relying on large public subsidies to maintain such institutions, a more effective form of financial support would be for governments to offer adequate scholarships to deserving graduate students and allow them to select an appropriate program of studies, either nationally or regionally.

Making Undergraduate and Professional Programs more Relevant

Efforts should be made to ensure that institutions' enrollment patterns and curricula reflect local skill requirements more closely. In many instances, this will mean shifting the balance of enrollments toward natural sciences and engineering. But in countries where enrollments in the applied sciences are too high—in Romania, for example, more than two-thirds of all university enrollments are in engineering and technical training—restructuring will need to establish courses in social sciences and management to ease the transition to a market economy. To guide the choice of course offerings and to make decisions on curriculum changes, institutions should monitor the labor market outcomes of their graduates, including placement and remuneration as well as the supply and demand of various skills. In the Philippines, the authorities publish the university board examination results for all engineering, medicine, dentistry, pharmacy, law, and accounting programs.

One way of achieving these goals is to promote the development of professional programs, either by creating new courses or by transforming existing programs. The duration of the professional programs should be determined by the requirements of the workplace rather than traditional academic criteria. A variety of relevant short programs (1–2 years) and long courses (3–5 years), as well as continuing education courses, can respond to rapidly changing needs for different types of skills. Introducing a modular curriculum associated with a credit system of academic organization allows for a greater number of specializations and more flexibility in course design.

In this connection, continuing education programs are not only important income-generating activities; they are also valuable in signaling changes in employment opportunities. Many institutions use continuing education programs to experiment with new courses and specializations. If there is sufficient student demand, these can be incorporated into full-time programs or provide the basis for new programs and electives. Continuing education programs, especially in fields like management, engineering, the health sciences, and education, are often staffed by individuals appointed on the basis of professional experience rather than academic credentials. This strengthens the relevance of the training and provides feedback from prospective employers. The many benefits of these programs are more apt to be realized when they are organized on a self-financing basis and when academic responsibility is exercised by faculties and departments.

Building Up External Linkages

An indigenous capacity for training and research is a necessary but not sufficient condition for higher education to contribute to growth. It needs to be complemented by science policies that include, in particular, mechanisms that promote better use of the scientific and technical potential of tertiary institutions (see box 5.3). Such mechanisms include both close linkages with industry in advanced training courses, cooperative research programs, consultancies, continuing education programs, science parks, and such benefits for industry as business incubation centers, tax advantages, and state-sponsored research vouchers. For example, Ghana's Technology Consultancy Centre in the University of Technology at Kumasi develops, promotes, and transfers appropriate technologies to small-scale industries. Jordan provides vouchers for small and medium-size enterprises to purchase research and development services from university. Taiwan (China)'s Hsinchu Science-Based Industrial Park and Korea's Daeduk City are developed in the vicinity of research universities and institutes to attract high technology firms to utilize the R&D capacity of higher education, and to make higher education more attuned to the needs of industry. A basic condition of success is the ability of the academic research community to forge links with non-university research institutes and enterprises and vice versa.

Many forms of cooperation between institutions and the productive sectors can be found throughout the developing world. Employers that actively define and design new curricula, monitor institutional management, organize student placement, and arrange for industry personnel to be seconded to tertiary institutions and for academic staff to have industrial experience, can contribute to aligning education to the country's needs and to the changing structure of the labor market. In all newly industrialized countries of East Asia, industrialists are consulted on both formal and informal basis on cur-

Establishing strong linkages between
the higher education system and the
economy is important to support
technology-based growth strategies.
In countries like Brazil and India, and
the former communist Eastern and
Central European countries, all of
which have had strong scientific and
technological research capacities for
decades, knowledge-driven industrial change has been impaired by a
lack of appropriate linkages with
training and research institutions.
The absence of market incentives to
introduce new products and processes or to improve production
methods has slowed down firm-
based technological accumulation
and hampered the appearance of
specialized suppliers. Training and
research institutions have operated
in isolation from industry.

By contrast, in Korea industrial
capacity was built using the graduates trained on a large scale in scientific and technical fields and by
promoting a close relationship between academic research and industry. The government provided
incentives to firms involved in tech-
nology-intensive exports coupled with
generous tax exemptions for research and development investments, thus creating a private sector
market for the products of its higher
education and science and technology systems.

Source: Eisemon 1992c.

ricula in higher education and R&D direction that can best serve the needs of
industry.

Pursuing Equity

Providing equitable opportunities for participation in higher education is an
important element of policies to increase national integration and the representation of traditionally disadvantaged groups in economic and political
leadership. Strategies must be multi-faceted if they are to be effective in
increasing the representation in higher education of women, ethnic minorities,
students from low-income families, and other economically or educationally
disadvantaged groups. Strategies include improving primary and secondary
education for these groups, increasing their demand for higher education,
diversifying institutions to serve various groups, subsidizing their studies, and
using admissions criteria to correct inequalities.

Improving the access of women, the poor, and other disadvantaged groups
to high-quality primary and secondary education is essential to any long-term
improvement in the equity of higher education. The distribution of enroll-

ments and the quality of instruction at the lower levels of education are the major determinants of representation in higher education. Demographic disparities cannot be remedied simply through corrective measures introduced at the higher level. They must be augmented by measures at the primary and secondary levels to reduce the variability in the performance of secondary school graduates and to enlarge the pool of eligible candidates.

Improving access to quality primary and secondary education will help stimulate demand over time. Other more immediate measures are also appropriate. Increasing women's demand for higher education, for instance, in part requires actions in labor market, fair employment, and family policies to make employment opportunities more attractive for women graduates. In part it also requires providing career information, role models of successful women, flexible modes of attendance (part-time studies, short courses, and credit systems) and separate facilities appropriate to cultural practices. Korea and Nigeria have arranged for female scientists, faculty members, and career counselors to visit secondary schools to discuss career opportunities. India built nine new polytechnics for women in 1991 and provides placement services to strengthen linkages with the labor market.

Diversifying institutions to serve the needs of different population groups can be effective. Different types of institutions have different equity effects in different countries. In India, open universities and distance education programs have benefited women, but have been less effective in increasing the participation of the disadvantaged scheduled caste and tribal students as well as those from rural areas. Thailand's two open universities have been the government's principal instrument for expanding access to the country's geographically well distributed but highly socially selective public university system. About a quarter (22 percent) of the students enrolled in these institutions come from rural areas, with the poorest social stratum accounting for two-thirds of the population. This is still much higher than the representation of students in public or private universities—11 percent and 10 percent, respectively—but it is well below their representation in teacher training institutions (52 percent), most of which are located in the countryside. Thai open universities have been much more important in increasing opportunities for students from poor family circumstances in urban areas (21 percent of enrollment, almost twice their representation in the general population).

The effectiveness of subsidies directed to underrepresented groups varies. Chile's competitive national scholarship scheme has increased the enrollment of students from the most educationally and economically disadvantaged backgrounds in the country's best public universities, while loans and expansion of private higher education generally have expanded opportunities for students from more advantaged families. Women's participation has been significantly increased through scholarships in Papua New Guinea and by providing boarding facilities in India and Yemen.

The most direct way to increase the representation in higher education of disadvantaged groups is to use meritocratic admissions criteria, which include relaxing requirements, awarding bonus points on entry examinations, imposing admissions quotas, and using combinations of these devices. These criteria are fraught with difficulties. Especially where the quality of secondary education is highly variable, they can involve high internal efficiency costs. In the early 1980s, for example, the public University of the Philippines decided to relax its rigorous admissions requirements for students from poor and rural families on the grounds that its entrance examinations underestimated the students' potential academic success. Students admitted under the scheme were given financial support and remedial instruction if needed and their performance was closely monitored. The results indicated that relaxing the requirements increased student failure despite the additional assistance the students received. In India, constitutionally mandated efforts to increase the representation of scheduled caste and tribal students through scholarships and reserved seat schemes have had a strong impact on the composition of higher education enrollments. Nevertheless, after four decades of positive discrimination in education and employment, scheduled caste and tribal groups remain seriously disadvantaged.

In many countries, admission to public universities is very selective and based on student achievement in national examinations that minimize qualitative variations at the secondary level. Minor adjustments in admissions requirements are unlikely to seriously affect the quality of entrants, but while the representation of particular groups may increase, their distribution across fields of study cannot be changed as easily. In Uganda, for example, bonus points were introduced in 1990 to increase the representation of women at Makerere University. The proportion of females admitted increased from 23 percent in 1989–90 to 30 percent in 1990–91, with women accounting for 40 percent of the arts intake but only 18 percent of the science intake. The relatively low representation of women among science students reflects the lack of science education for women at the secondary level and cannot be remedied at the higher education level alone. Hence, as noted above, equity must be increased at the primary and secondary levels as part of any long-term program also to increase it in higher education.

CHAPTER SIX

Implications for the World Bank

ALTHOUGH loans and grants from external aid and lending agencies may be marginal to the overall cost of financing higher education, they are often crucial to the institutions that receive them. Such support is a channel through which developing countries and economies in transition can gain access to the resources and expertise of the educational, scientific, and intellectual centers of more industrialized countries (see box 6.1).

Since 1963, the World Bank has had a prominent role in assisting the expansion of post-secondary education. Investments averaged 17 percent of total lending for education between 1963 and 1970, peaked at 38 percent between 1971 and 1985, and represented 31 percent between 1986 and 1993. In all, 294 projects with 457 higher education components have been supported, representing a $5.7 billion investment during the past thirty years (billion is defined here as 1,000 million). Most of this investment ($5.1 billion) has occurred since 1980 (see table 6.1).

Initially, World Bank lending for higher education was mainly directed toward institutions that train professionals and technicians for the economy or to teachers to facilitate expansion of lower levels of education. The first higher education project (in Pakistan, 1964) helped establish two agricultural universities. In recent years, the World Bank has increasingly provided support to universities and institutions responsible for advanced scientific train-

---

**BOX 6.1 SUPPORT BY
EXTERNAL AID AND LENDING
AGENCIES FOR HIGHER
EDUCATION**

A 1992 survey of educational assistance to seventeen Latin American, Caribbean, African, and Asian countries indicated that assistance for university development (excluding untargeted funding for overseas training) typically accounted for only 1 to 2 percent of total development assistance. The proportion of educational assistance allocated for higher education was greatest in African countries; for example, the figure for Burundi was 61 percent. Foreign training accounted for a very large share of higher education assistance, again especially in African countries: 69 percent in Cameroon, 51 percent in Kenya, and 72 percent in Nigeria.

Patterns of involvement by external aid and lending agencies in higher education once reflected historical, usually colonial, relationships or were circumscribed by the language adopted for higher education by the recipient country. That is no longer

the case. Only in Burundi, Nigeria, and Senegal, do the former metropolitan countries predominate among external agencies supporting higher education. Germany was the leading supporter in India, Sweden in Zimbabwe, Japan in Kenya, and the United States in Cameroon. Italy is a major supporter of higher education in two anglophone African countries, Kenya and Nigeria.

Higher education is both an object of external agency support and an implementing modality for agricultural, health, population, and other sectoral assistance. Most support for staff upgrading, technical assistance, rehabilitation of facilities, and the purchase of library materials or laboratory equipment is highly targeted, short-term, and focused on the needs of academic units. Indirect assistance to university education was very substantial in many of the countries studied. In Thailand, for instance, 49 percent of support for university education was embedded in other sectoral assistance.

Source: Eisemon and Kourouma 1992.

---

ing and research, reflecting their centrality to knowledge-based economic growth strategies. African and East Asian countries have had the largest number of higher education investments, and Latin America and the Caribbean countries the lowest.

The relative share of higher education lending in each region reflects differences in priorities set at the country level. The volume of lending is indicative of specific circumstances such as the economic situation and the human resources development strategy of borrowing countries. A small number of countries in each region have received most of the financing that the

TABLE 6.1 WORLD BANK LENDING FOR HIGHER EDUCATION BY REGION, 1980–93
(number of institutions, lending in millions of dollars, percentage of Bank lending)

Institution	Africa	East Asia	South Asia	Middle East and North Africa	Europe and Central Asia	Latin America and the Caribbean	Total
University	32,	25,	4,	15,	3,	5,	83,
	342,	1,457,	31,	135,	84,	80,	2,131,
	6.7	28.6	0.6	2.7	1.7	1.6	41.9
Science and	1,	11,	0,	4,	2,	3,	24,
technology	11,	475,	0,	65,	40,	391,	983,
	0.2	9.3	0.0	1.3	0.8	7.7	19.3
Polytechnics	4,	5,	6,	5,	1,	3,	24,
	36,	197,	539,	9,	4,	7,	794,
	0.7	3.9	10.6	0.2	0.1	0.1	15.6
Technical	21,	8,	4,	9,	3,	3,	48,
institutes	83,	246,	37,	96,	121,	11,	596,
	1.6	4.8	0.7	1.9	2.4	0.2	11.7
Teacher	26,	24,	6,	21,	2,	7,	86,
training	69,	378,	28,	91,	5,	11,	584,
institutions	1.4	7.4	0.6	1.8	0.1	0.2	11.5
Total	83,	73,	20,	54,	11,	21,	262,
project	542,	2,754,	637,	397,	254,	502,	5,089,
components	10.7	54.1	12.5	7.8	5.0	9.9	100

Source: World Bank data.

Bank has made available for higher education. These typically have large higher education systems whose expansion or rehabilitation requires large investments. Since 1986, Nigeria has been Africa's leading borrower for higher education, China and Indonesia have been East Asia's, Brazil has been Latin America's, and Hungary has been Europe's.

The World Bank has accumulated a great deal of lending experience in supporting different kinds of higher education institutions in many countries between 1980 and 1993. It has had projects supporting three or more types of institutions in 29 African countries, 16 Latin American and Caribbean countries, 8 Middle Eastern and European countries, 5 South Asian countries, 11 East Asian countries, and 3 European and Central Asian countries. In several countries, Algeria, Brazil, China, Indonesia, the Philippines, and Portugal, the Bank has supported universities, science and technology institutes, polytechnics, technical institutes, and teacher training colleges.

Lessons from Experience

Support for quality improvement in World Bank projects has often been provided piecemeal, with a narrow focus on discrete teaching and research activities. This has constrained the impact of these investments. Assistance to libraries and laboratories, as well as for training, staff research, and other purposes, has occasionally created well-funded academic oases that became unsustainable in the long run. For example, supplying laboratory equipment for instruction and staff research can have only a limited impact if there are no funds to replenish consumables. New libraries and classroom facilities will not be maintained if professional and support staff must seek other employment in order to sustain themselves. In Indonesia, for instance, World Bank support for higher education has had mixed results, mainly for lack of a well-defined policy framework for the subsector. Sixteen Inter-University Centers (IUCs) for advanced scientific training and research in strategic fields like biotechnology were established in the late 1980s with World Bank assistance. They were situated at Indonesia's leading public universities and received funding for buildings, laboratories, equipment, overseas training of staff, foreign technical assistance, and staff research. Although the number of postgraduate degrees (48 doctoral and 253 master's) increased between 1985 and 1990, the research output of the centers was disappointing. Few mainstream scientific papers had been produced. Indonesian researchers received some payment for their work at the IUCs, but the amounts were not sufficient to enable many of them to give up their second jobs. As a result, research efforts were conducted on a part-time basis. In contrast, the bonuses given to staff to supervise theses and dissertations has significantly increased the output of graduate students and led to pressures to proliferate graduate programs in the public universities.

The interrelatedness of academic programs and institutions of higher education has seldom been taken into consideration. Advanced scientific training and research requires strong undergraduate programs. High-quality instruction in engineering, medicine, agriculture and applied social sciences is built on sound training in the natural sciences, mathematics, and even the humanities whose importance to economic development is less obvious, and thus less apt to attract support from external agencies. In brief, whole institutions and systems of higher education must be strengthened to produce sustainable improvements. Furthermore, the World Bank has not always been able to offer the long-term comprehensive support for higher education institutions that is usually needed for effective institution building.

A World Bank internal review of implementation experience undertaken in 1992 concluded that Bank lending for higher education has been most successful where, through a series of complementary project investments, it has developed a subsectoral strategy for intervention. In China, for example, loans have involved different tiers of the subsector in ways that have strengthened the higher education system as a whole and addressed equity and quality issues in a comprehensive manner (see box 6.2).

The three decades of World Bank education lending to the Republic of Korea offer another example of a successful approach, which involved well-integrated support for investments to develop the national scientific training and research infrastructure as well as industrial capacities. After providing funding for agricultural colleges and various technical institutions throughout the 1970s, the Bank supported efforts to expand training in management and engineering, including the establishment of an accrediting body for engineering education, during the 1980s. Four more projects were approved between 1989 and 1991 to reinforce advanced scientific training and research capacities in both the public and private sectors and to strengthen links between science and technology producing institutions and industrial users. World Bank lending for higher education in Korea has corresponded with Korea's push for high technology development in the 1980s and 1990s, and has been complemented by lending for technology development and transfer.

In Sub-Saharan Africa, higher education has featured prominently in recent policy-based lending operations. Since 1986, education sector adjustment loans to ten Sub-Saharan African countries have included higher education reform measures. In all ten countries these reforms have focused on containing or reducing public expenditures for degree-granting higher education institutions, combining restrictions on enrollment growth with lower per-student grants and subsidies as well as the introduction of a variety of cost-recovery measures. The cost-containment strategy has often been complemented by reforms designed to increase internal efficiency by, for instance, increasing student-staff ratios or teaching loads. However, in less than half of these cases have investments been made in the higher education subsector in order to facilitate reforms.

Designing politically acceptable and fiscally affordable policy reform has been difficult, and implementation experience is not encouraging. Reform implementation has been opposed by various interest groups and has touched off student rioting in many countries. The successful launching and imple-

BOX 6.2 SUPPORTING HIGHER EDUCATION DEVELOPMENT IN CHINA

Support for higher education development in China has occurred through a series of integrated project loans involving different tiers of the higher education subsector. Within the framework of China's Four Modernizations Plan of 1980, the World Bank began by assisting the country's elite national universities, whose programs had been disrupted by the Cultural Revolution. World Bank funding facilitated construction and/or rehabilitation of university libraries and laboratories, updating of instructional and research programs with foreign scientific expert assistance, and upgrading of academic staff's professional qualifications through foreign training. Later projects addressed the needs of the provincial universities and other kinds of institutions of higher education, while the most recent focus, again on national institutions, directed efforts toward advanced scientific research and training.

Reviewing the World Bank's program of assistance to Chinese higher education in the 1980s, an independent research work noted that:

Approximately 183 higher institutions in the formal system, out of the 1985 total of 1,016 regular institutions, were included in these projects: 30 universities under the ministry

mentation of reforms and innovations is conditioned by the ability of decision-makers to build a consensus among the various constituents of the higher education subsector. Cost containment, cost recovery, and internal efficiency reforms must confer tangible benefits to governments and universities and be introduced in the context of more fundamental reforms that affect the autonomy and financing of institutions. This is currently being tried in Viet Nam.

Guidelines for Future Lending

Higher education investments are important for economic growth. They increase individuals' productivity and incomes, as indicated by rate-of-return analysis, and they also produce significant external benefits not captured by rate-of-return analysis, such as the long-term returns from basic research and from technology development and transfer. Economic growth is a critical prerequisite for sustained poverty reduction in developing countries, which is the overarching objective of the World Bank.

Within the education sector, however, there is evidence that higher educa-

of education (now the State Education Commission), 34 under a range of other national ministries, 32 under agriculture and forestry (including 13 provincial), 14 under public health, 56 at the provincial level, and 17 short-cycle vocational universities administered by city governments . . . Its outstanding feature was the broad spread of assistance, in which no major sector of the higher education system was neglected. [Hayhoe 1989]

Over the course of a decade and through eight investment projects aimed at increasing quality, access, and efficiency at approximately two hundred national, provincial, and municipal universities, as well as various technical, vocational, and scientific institutions, China's higher education system has been strengthened considerably. World Bank assistance has facilitated China's reentry into the international mainstream in many fields of scientific training and research. The World Bank, in return, has acquired experience throughout the higher education subsector, an understanding of how its different tiers are related to each other, and has become better able to target its lending to key training and research programs.

Sources: International Advisory Panel and Chinese Review Commission 1991; Hayhoe 1989; Frame and Narin 1987; Eisemon 1992c.

---

tion investments have lower social rates of return than investments in primary and secondary education and that investments in basic education can also have a more direct impact on poverty reduction, because they tend to improve income equality. Recognizing this, developing countries throughout the world are investing heavily at these levels, and in primary education in particular; gross primary enrollment ratios increased from 79 percent to 104 percent between 1970 and 1990. This progress has been supported with World Bank lending, and primary and secondary education will continue to be the highest-priority subsectors in the Bank's education lending to countries that have not yet achieved universal literacy and adequate access, equity, and quality at the primary and secondary levels. In these countries, the Bank's involvement in higher education will continue to be mainly to make its financing more equitable and cost-effective, so that primary and secondary education can receive increased attention at the margin.

Reform of higher education, and particularly strategies for mobilizing greater private financing for higher education through cost-sharing and the promotion of private institutions, can help countries free up some of the incremental public resources needed to improve quality and access at the primary and secondary levels. World Bank lending for higher education thus has a further strong justification: to support countries' efforts to adopt policy reforms that will allow the subsector to operate more efficiently and at lower public cost. Countries prepared to adopt a higher education policy framework that stresses a differentiated institutional structure and diversified resource base, with greater emphasis on private providers and private funding, will continue to receive priority. In these countries, Bank lending for higher education is supporting:

- Sector policy reforms
- Institutional development
- Quality improvement.

Supporting Sector Policy Reforms

World Bank lending is increasingly designed to support reforms of financial and managerial policies necessary to establish a more equitable, efficient, and higher-quality system.

Bank lending in support of reform programs can include financing for investments as well as the implementation of policy measures. While the composition of the package of policy reforms will vary by region and income level, reflecting the specific socioeconomic and political circumstances of each country, in most cases it includes some combination of measures to:

- Control access to public higher education on the basis of efficient and equitable selection criteria
- Encourage the development of institutions with different programs and different missions
- Establish a positive environment for private institutions
- Introduce or increase cost-sharing and other financial diversification measures
- Provide loan, grant, and work-study programs to ensure that all qualified but financially needy students can pursue higher education
- Allocate public resources to higher education transparently and in ways that strengthen quality and increase efficiency
- Enable higher education institutions to autonomously raise and utilize resources and determine student intake.

The World Bank will continue to adapt its lending strategy and policy dialogue in higher education to different regional requirements. No package of policy reforms can be effective in all circumstances, nor can all necessary reforms be implemented simultaneously. But any package will need to be monitorable and to demonstrate progress toward financial sustainability. Strengthening the policy environment to improve higher education performance is a long-term process that the Bank supports with analytical expertise and lending.

Capacity Building and Institutional Development

Capacity building and institutional development for higher education need to be supported by the World Bank at both the national and institutional levels.

National Level

Support for capacity building will continue to be directed toward strengthening the capacity of the government for policymaking and coordinating reform implementation. This often implies Bank assistance in strengthening oversight or advisory bodies with a capacity for policy analysis, evaluation of requests for funding, monitoring institutions' performance and making information about institutions' performance available to students. It can also include support for establishing transparent mechanisms to guide government allocation of public spending on higher education institutions.

The Bank has supported such capacity building initiatives in Kenya, Mauritius, Romania, Uganda, and elsewhere, providing expert assistance when necessary and financial support for technical studies. In Mauritius, for example, the Bank supported government efforts to establish a tertiary education commission, whose first task was to prepare a master plan for the rationalization and development of the higher education sector. Technical assistance was made available to assist each of the four tertiary institutions in preparing an institutional development plan (IDP). Each IDP defined the specific mission of the institution, its development goals, an academic plan, and the resources needed to achieve these objectives. The next step was to integrate the IDPs into a coherent development plan for the whole subsector.

An increasingly high priority area for Bank support is assisting countries to set up or restructure student loan and financial assistance systems. As strategies to expand cost-sharing are pursued, well-functioning loan and grant schemes become essential for ensuring equity of access to higher education. An example of this type of assistance is the recently approved student loan reform project in Venezuela, which supports the recapitalization, computerization, and administrative strengthening of the key student loan agency in conjunction with policy reforms to increase real interest rates on student loans and improve loan recovery.

Institutional Level

At the institutional level, the World Bank will continue to offer assistance to strengthen the managerial capacity of universities and other institutions and their ability to achieve efficiency gains through effective planning, sound financial management, and improved program delivery. In Mozambique, for example, the Bank is supporting Eduardo Mondlane University's institutional development program. The Bank program is improving instruction by providing textbooks and study materials; reducing staff losses by providing access to housing and supporting professional training of both academic and administrative staff; improving management and accountability by providing short-term management training linked to staff development and by contracting an annual external audit; ensuring adequate regional and gender representation by increasing student housing; and restoring the physical plant by instituting a maintenance program.

Such interventions have been useful for generating debate on policy reforms as well as for mobilizing external resources. For example, an eighteen-month internal study conducted by Eduardo Mondlane University to establish objectives and priorities for long-term development has been the basis for its discussions with the community of aid and lending agencies in garnering support for its projects.

Improving Quality

National strategies for higher education development that include an explicit focus on improving the quality of instruction and research will continue to receive priority World Bank support in countries that have undertaken appropriate policy reforms. The Bank typically assists governments in implementing the necessary policy reforms in conjunction with a series of projects that support quality improvements in universities and other institutions. These investments take place within a sectorwide strategy to reform higher education as a whole.

Insofar as universities are concerned, priority is increasingly given to concentrating resources in a few institutions, either public or private, providing undergraduate education in fields of importance to the country's human resource development, and offering advanced scientific training and producing research of an international standard. An increasing share of World Bank investments in higher education is therefore targeted to support national and regional centers of excellence. To develop or strengthen institutional centers of excellence in small nations, support for regional initiatives is expanding along the lines described in chapter 5. This includes support for national institutions operating as regional centers rather than the creation of new supra-national institutions. Aid can involve direct assistance to national institutions or programs with a regional mission, such as staff development or equipment upgrading, and national programs of scholarships for students attending regional institutions outside their country of origin.

More specifically, the World Bank is giving increasing priority to investments designed to enhance the quality of instruction and research by providing assistance for:

- Upgrading the qualifications of academic staff
- Introducing innovations in teaching, the organization and content of academic programs, and methods of assessing student performance
- Increasing the provision and quality of instructional facilities and resources to support institutional plans for self-improvement
- Improving examinations and selection processes
- Establishing accreditation and performance assessment systems
- Increasing the productivity and quality of graduate training and staff research, including support for national and international scientific communication.

The World Bank is increasingly providing funding to higher education institutions on a competitive basis, in a way analogous to its support for university research in Brazil, China, and Korea. In Hungary, for example, the Bank is assisting rationalization and reform of the higher education and research system through a fund for new initiatives (see box 6.3). Access to this fund is competitive, and grants are made to institutions to strengthen the quality, efficiency, and relevance of their programs. Proposals are reviewed by expert panels, and medium-term support is provided to facilitate innovations. The scheme is integral to the success of the reforms needed to ensure the sustainability of these initiatives. Similarly, the ongoing engineering education project in Egypt provides funds to rehabilitate and construct new facilities, purchase laboratory equipment and library materials, and support staff development programs. Funding is awarded after a review of proposals for self-improvement that are prepared by engineering departments from internal self-audits of their needs and reform plans.

The Bank is also supporting efforts to differentiate higher education systems. This can include funding for short-cycle and continuing education pro-

BOX 6.3 SUPPORTING STRUCTURAL REFORMS IN HUNGARY

A major reform of higher education now being implemented in Hungary will change the way most higher education institutions are financed, including research institutes that provide advanced scientific training. A new higher education law, presented to the national parliament in 1992, reorganized the public higher education system, legitimized the establishment of private institutions, allowed public institutions to levy fees, changed the procedures for allocating state support to students and institutions, created funds to support research, institutional rehabilitation, and innovation, and established new policy structures to direct the growth of the higher education system. The reforms are being supported by a World Bank loan (1991).

The higher education law brings all higher education within the authority of one ministry, which will be advised by a committee for higher education and research. The committee will be composed of representatives of the various ministries concerned with higher education, university rectors and administrators of scientific institutions, and local and foreign experts. It will formulate norms for financing public and private institutions and make recommendations through the ministry to parliament on public expenditures for higher education.

Support will be distributed to institutions and their students through various funds. Students will receive payments from the state student fund for part of the costs of accommodation, boarding, and textbooks and, in addition, will receive loans to pay these and other costs interest-free for ten years. A tuition fund will provide support to institutions based on their efficiency and performance as well as the costs of the programs they offer. The higher education research fund will selectively support proposals from institutions that fall outside the mandate of other national research councils, while the facilities fund can be accessed by institutions for extraordinary capital needs. Universities and colleges will be allowed to determine and allocate intake except in the case of certain professional faculties such as medicine, dentistry, and veterinary medicine, whose enrollment will be controlled by the committee for higher education and research. The institutions will be allowed to obtain additional income from private sources without reduction of their operating budgets, set salaries and wages of academic and nonacademic staff, and manipulate other aspects of their cost structure subject to minimum accrediting standards adopted by the committee to determine eligibility for support from the tuition fund.

Source: Hungary 1991.

grams, open universities, and diploma- and certificate-granting institutions, as well as establishing and expanding private higher education. Most of the future increase in higher education enrollments will be absorbed by these institutions. For this purpose, World Bank investments are more and more directed at improving the quality of training offered by these institutions.

Findings of the World Bank's Operations Evaluation Department

LITTLE has been done in the past to evaluate the World Bank's work on higher education in a comprehensive way. The Bank's Operations Evaluation Department (OED) has evaluated higher education projects in their 1978 "Review of Bank Operations in the Education Sector" and more recently in "World Bank Assistance to Agricultural Higher Education 1964–1990" (World Bank 1992f) and a 1991 report on "Indonesian Education and the World Bank: An Assessment of Two Decades of Lending" (World Bank 1991a). In addition, some projects have been assessed in the "Annual Review of Project Performance Results" from 1985 to 1987 and "Annual Review of Evaluation Results" from 1988 to 1991. Review of these documents shows that the Bank started financing higher education institutions in 1963 on the assumption that these institutions would supply the trained labor power and adapt the new technologies necessary to enhance economic development.

Financing in the early years emphasized hardware, such as construction and equipment, with a gradual shift to supporting improved software, such as teacher training and new methods of delivering educational services. The 1978 report, which encompasses the years 1963 to 1978, reviewed a total of 55 education projects and covered all subsectors. The main thrust of these projects was to achieve expansion—only 3 percent of which was in higher education—as well as to bring about improvements in administration and planning, in teaching facilities, and in the training and status of teachers in education in general. In the late 1960s to early 1970s two main objectives of the higher education projects were to direct universities towards research on local problems and to encourage the expansion of training in science and technology. Many projects were designed to assist multiple subsectors so that allocations to higher education represented only a small slice of the total. For example, for agricultural projects between 1964 and 1990, while total project costs were estimated to be $2,840 million ($2.84 billion), the cost of the agricultural higher education components was only $715 million, with Asia receiving 80 percent of the total investment. The majority of higher education projects assisted one or two institutions in a particular country.

Several problems were identified. The first was the failure to understand universities as complex and unique organizations—the planning did not take into account whether projects were sustainable, how the institutional structure would mix with the socioeconomic and the political environment, or how internal academic politics would affect the project. With agricultural higher education projects in particular, little thought was given to commitment on the part of the borrower. The second problem was weak analysis of issues on the basis of unrealistic labor market assessments due in part to the absence of comprehensive labor market data. Unworkable implementation arrangements were also a recurrent problem.

Over the period under review, projects increasingly stressed enhancing university management—improving resource allocation and internal efficiency, rationalizing program development, and controlling the growth of recurrent expenditures. With regard to implementation, some projects suffered from time and cost overruns. Implementation lags did not necessarily result in adverse outcomes, however. The bulk of the implementation problems arose from implementation arrangements that did not allow for autonomous execution of the component and did not involve university staff sufficiently; supervision by Bank staff who were unfamiliar with higher education issues; poor performance by technical assistance experts; and weak monitoring and evaluation systems that were not able to identify and correct problems as they occurred. This was especially evident in Indonesia, the Bank's largest and most diversified education program ever undertaken.

Overall, projects usually achieved their targets for expanding facilities, improving the physical plant, and upgrading staff, and enrollments were generally in line with expectations. Less impressive were the results pertaining to the impact of projects on broader institutional objectives and economic development.

A 1993 OED report on "The World Bank Role in Human Resource Development in Sub-Saharan Africa" (World Bank 1993) stressed that the situation of African universities has become dramatic and that the continent continues to be heavily dependent on expatriate experts. In recent years, Bank lending has concentrated on primary education, resulting in the relative neglect of African higher education. In addition, Bank projects in that subsector have favored support for teacher training over investment in universities. The report noted that too much faith has been put in the results of conventional rates of return analysis, which led to the recommendation to reallocate resources from higher education to the lower levels of education. Given the methodological limitations of that approach, and the importance of higher education for producing the professional and technical specialists required by each country, the report called for increased Bank attention to the needs of African higher education institutions. It also recommended, for reasons of political feasibility, a more consultative approach in the preparation of projects to support higher education reforms.

Selected Bibliography

Adams, Arvil V., John Middleton, and Adrian Ziderman. "Market-based Manpower Planning with Labour Market Signals." *International Labor Review* 131(3): 261–80.

Albornoz, Orlando. 1992. "Government and Higher Education in Developing Countries: The Venezuelan Case." World Bank, Education and Social Policy Department, Washington, D.C.

Albrecht, Douglas, and Adrian Ziderman. 1992a. *Deferred Cost Recovery for Higher Education: Student Loan Programs in Developing Countries*. World Bank Discussion Paper 137. Washington, D.C.

———. 1992b. "Financing Higher Education in Developing Countries." World Bank, Population and Human Resources Department, Education and Employment Division Background Paper Series PHREE/92/61. Washington, D.C.

———. 1992c. *Funding Mechanisms for Higher Education: Financing for Stability, Efficiency and Responsiveness*. World Bank Discussion Paper 153. Washington, D.C.

Bacchus, M. K. 1992. "Key Issues in the Provision of Higher Education in Small Nation States." Paper prepared for World Bank Small States Policy Seminar on Higher Education, Negara Brunei Darussalam, June 14–18. World Bank, Education and Social Policy Department, Washington, D.C.

Bell, Martin, and Keith Pavitt. 1992. "Accumulating Technological Capability in Developing Countries." *Proceedings of the World Bank Annual Conference on Development Economics 1992*, 257–81. Washington, D.C.: World Bank.

Bellew, Rosemary and Joseph DeStefano. 1991. "Costs and Finance of Higher Education in Pakistan." Policy, Research, and External Affairs Working Paper WPS704. World Bank, Education and Social Policy Department, Washington, D.C.

Blair, R. D. D. 1991. "An Assessment of Progress and the Potential for Financial Diversification and Income Generation at Selected African Universities." World Bank, Human Resources Division, Technical Department, Africa Region, Washington, D.C.

Blomqvist, Ake. 1986. *Higher Education and the Markets for Educated Labor in LDCS: Theoretical Approaches and Implications.* London, Canada: University of Western Ontario.

Bray, Mark. 1990. "Provision of Higher Education in Small States: Demands, Constraints and Strategies." *Higher Education Quarterly* 44(3): 264–81.

Brunner, José Joaquin. 1992. "Government and Higher Education in Chile." World Bank, Education and Social Policy Department, Washington, D.C.

Brunner, José Joaquin, and Guillermo Briones. 1992. "Higher Education in Chile: Effects of the 1980 Reform." World Bank, Education and Social Policy Department, Washington, D.C.

Carlson, Samuel. 1992. "Private Financing of Higher Education in Latin America and the Caribbean." World Bank, Latin America and the Caribbean Technical Department Regional Studies Program, Report 18. Washington D.C.

Carnoy, Martin. 1992. "Universities, Technological Change, and Training in the Information Age." Paper prepared for the World Bank Senior Policy Seminar on Strengthening Public and Private Roles in Asian Higher Education, Singapore, June 28–July 3. World Bank, Education and Social Policy Department, Washington, D.C.

Castells, Manuel. 1991. "The University System: Engine of Development in the New World Economy." Paper prepared for the World Bank Worldwide Seminar on Higher Education and Development," Kuala Lumpur, June. World Bank, Education and Social Policy Department, Washington, D.C.

Clark, Burton. 1990. "Is California the Model for OECD Futures?" Paper presented at 1990 meeting on the 1989 OECD Review of Higher Education Policy in California. Los Angeles: Clark Kerr Center.

———. 1991. "A Classification of Systems and Institutions of Higher Education." World Bank, Education and Social Policy Department, Washington, D.C.

Coffman, James. 1991. "Algerian Higher Education: A Field Researcher's Comments on the State of the Institution and Its Future." School of Education, Stanford University, Palo Alto, Calif.

Coward, H. Roberts. 1990. *Literature-Based Indicator Techniques for Profiling Science and Technology Infrastructure in Developing Countries.* Economics of Technology Working Paper 4. Arlington, Va.: SRI International Science and Technology Policy Program.

Dahlman, Carl, and Frischtak, Claudio. 1990. "National Systems Supporting Technical Advance in Industry: The Brazilian Experience." Industry Series Paper 32. World Bank, Industry and Energy Department, Washington D.C.

dePietro-Jurand, Robin. 1993. "Women's Access to Higher Education: A Review of the Literature." World Bank, Education and Social Policy Department, Washington, D.C.

DeStefano, Joseph, and Rosemary Rinaldi. 1990. "World Bank Lending for University Education: A General Operational Review." World Bank, Education and Social Policy Department, Washington, D.C.

Eisemon, Thomas. 1992a. "Higher Education and the State in Uganda." World Bank, Education and Social Policy Department, Washington, D.C.

————. 1992b. "Language Issues in Scientific Training and Research in Developing Countries." World Bank, Population and Human Resources Department, Education and Employment Division Background Paper Series PHREE/92/47. Washington, D.C.

————. 1992c. "Lending for Higher Education: An Analysis of World Bank Investment 1963-1991." World Bank, Population and Human Resources Department, Education and Employment Division Background Paper Series PHREE/92/66R. Washington, D.C.

————. 1992d. "Private Initiatives and Traditions of State Control in Higher Education in Sub-Saharan Africa." World Bank, Population and Human Resources Department, Education and Employment Division Background Paper Series PHREE/92/48. Washington, D.C.

Eisemon, Thomas, and Charles Davis. 1989. "Publication Strategies in Four Peripheral Asian Scientific Communities: Some Issues in the Measurement and Interpretation of Non-Mainstream Science." In Philip Altbach, Charles H. Davis, Thomas O. Eisemon, S. Gopinathan, H. Steve Hsieh, Sungho Lee, Pangen Fong, and Jasbir Sarjit Singh, eds., *Scientific Development and Higher Education in Newly Industrialized Countries*. New York: Praeger Publishers.

————. 1992. "Universities and Scientific Research Capacity." *Journal of Asian and African Studies* 27(3): 69–94.

Eisemon, Thomas, and Moussa Kourouma. 1992. "Foreign Assistance for University Development in Sub-Saharan Africa and Asia." World Bank, Education and Social Policy Department, Washington, D.C.

Eisemon, Thomas, and Jamil Salmi. 1993. "African Universities and the State: Prospects for Reform in Senegal and Uganda." *Higher Education* 25 (2): 151–68.

Eisemon, Thomas, John Sheehan, George Eyoku, Franklin Van Buer, Delane Welsch, Louisa Masutti, Nat Colletta, and Lee Roberts. 1993. "Strengthening Uganda's Policy for Investing in University Development." World Bank, Population and Human Resources Department Working Paper WPS 1065. Washington, D.C.

Enos, J. L. and W. H. Park. 1988. *The Adoption and Diffusion of Imported Technology: The Case of Korea*. London: Croom Helm.

Fagerberg, Jan. 1988. "International Competitiveness." *Economic Journal: The Journal of the Royal Economic Society*, 98(June): 355–74.

Fielden, John. 1991. "Improving Management Practice in Higher Education in Developing Countries." World Bank, Education and Social Policy Department, Washington, D.C.

Frame, J. D., and R. Narin. 1987. "The Growth of Chinese Scientific Research." *Scientometrics* 12: 135–44.

Geiger, Roger. 1986. *Private Sectors in Higher Education: Structure, Function and Change in Eight Countries*. Ann Arbor: University of Michigan Press.

Gonzalez, Andrew. 1992. "Government and Higher Education in Developing Countries: The Philippines." World Bank, Education and Social Policy Department, Washington, D.C.

Gopinathan, S. 1992. "Higher Education in Singapore: A Study of Policy, Development, Financing and Governance 1960–1990." World Bank, Education and Social Policy Department, Washington, D.C.

Greene, J. Edward. 1992. "Policy Options in Higher Education for Small States with Special Reference to the University of the West Indies." Paper prepared for the World Bank Small States Policy Seminar on Higher Education, Negara Brunei Darussalam, June 14–18. World Bank, Education and Social Policy Department, Washington, D.C.

Guin, Jacques. 1992. "Nouveaux Défis à l'Enseignement Supérieur: Qualité et Resources." Paper presented at World Bank Regional Seminar on Higher Education, Harare, Zimbabwe. World Bank, Education and Social Policy Department, Washington, D.C.

Hanson, Philip, and Keith Pavitt. 1987. *The Comparative Economics of Research, Development and Innovation in East and West: A Survey*. New York: Harwood Academic Publishers.

Hayhoe, Ruth. 1989. *China's Universities and the Open Door*. Armonk, N.Y.: M. E. Sharpe.

Hinchcliffe, Keith. 1985. *Issues Related to Higher Education in Sub-Saharan Africa*. World Bank Staff Working Paper 780. Washington, D.C.

Hungary, Government of. 1991. *Concept for Higher Education Development in Hungary*. Budapest: Coordination Office of Higher Education.

International Advisory Panel and Chinese Review Commission. 1991. *Evaluation Report: Chinese University Development Project II*. Washington, D.C.: National Academy Press.

Islamic Azad University. 1992. *Islamic Azad University*. Tehran.

Jaffe, Adam. 1989. "Real Effects of Academic Research." *American Economic Review* 79(December): 957–70.

James, Estelle. 1986. "Cross-Subsidization in Higher Education: Does It Pervert Private Choice and Public Policy?" In Daniel Levy, ed., *Private Education: Studies in Choice and Public Policy*. New York: Oxford University Press.

Johnstone, D. Bruce. 1992. "Public and Private Financing Strategies for Higher Education in Asia." Paper prepared for the World Bank Senior Policy Seminar on Strengthening Public and Private Roles in Asian Higher Education, Singapore, June 28–July 3. World Bank, Education and Social Policy Department, Washington, D.C.

Kaneko, Motohisa. 1992. "A Comparative Study of Higher Education Development in Selected Asian Countries 1960–1990: Country Case Study: Japan." World Bank, Asia Technical Department, Population and Human Resources Division, Washington, D.C.

Kells, Herbert R. 1991. "Performance Indicators for Higher Education: A Critical

Review with Policy Recommendations." World Bank, Population and Human Resources Department, Education and Employment Division Background Paper Series PHREE/92/56. Washington, D.C.

Kim, Ransoo. 1992. "A Comparative Study of Higher Education Development in Selected Asian Countries 1960–1990: A Country Case Study of Higher Education in Korea." World Bank, Asia Technical Department, Population and Human Resources Division, Washington, D.C.

Klitgaard, Robert. 1986. *Elitism and Meritocracy in Developing Countries: Selection Policy for Higher Education*. Baltimore, Md.: Johns Hopkins University Press.

Kornhauser, Aleksandra. 1992. "University-Industry Cooperation under Constraints: Experience of the International Center for Chemical Studies, Ljubljana, Slovenia." World Bank, Population and Human Resources Department, Education and Employment Division Background Paper Series PHREE/92/67. Washington, D.C.

Leslie, Larry, and Paul Brinkman. 1988. *The Economic Value of Higher Education*. New York: Macmillan.

Levy, Daniel. 1986. *Higher Education and the State: Private Challenges to Public Dominance*. Chicago: University of Chicago Press.

———. 1991. "Problems of Privatization." Paper presented at the World Bank Seminar on Innovation and Improvement of Higher Education in Developing Countries, Kuala Lumpur, Malaysia. June 30–July 4. World Bank, Education and Social Policy Department, Washington, D.C.

———. 1992. "Towards State Supervision? Changing Patterns of Governance in Mexican Higher Education." World Bank, Education and Social Policy Department, Washington, D.C.

Lockheed, Marlaine, E. John Middleton, and Greta Nettleton, eds. 1991. Educational Technology: Sustainable and Effective Use. World Bank, Population and Human Resources Department, Education and Employment Division, Background Paper Series PHREE/91/32. Washington, D.C.

McMahon, Walter W., and Boediono. 1992. *Education and the Economy: The External Efficiency of Education*. Jakarta, Indonesia: Ministry of Education and Culture.

Majumdar, Tapas. 1992. "Higher Education in India: Development, Financing and Governance: 1960–1990." World Bank, Education and Social Policy Department, Washington, D.C.

Manrakhan, Jagadish. 1992. "On Matters Related to the Brain Drain in Small States: The Mauritian Experience." Paper prepared for the World Bank Small States Policy Seminar on Higher Education, Negara Brunei Darussalam, June 14–18. World Bank, Education and Social Policy Department, Washington, D.C.

Mansfield, Edwin. 1992a. "Academic Research and Industrial Innovation." *Research Policy* 20 (Feb.): 1–12.

———. 1992b. "Economic Returns from Investment in Research and Training." World Bank, Education and Social Policy Department, Washington, D.C.

Marimuthu, T., and S. Abraham. 1992. "Higher Education in Malaysia." World Bank, Education and Social Policy Department, Washington, D.C.

Marquis, Carlos. 1992. "Argentine Federal Government and the Universities." World Bank, Education and Social Policy Department, Washington, D.C.

Maxwell, Ian. 1980. *Universities in Partnership*. Edinburgh: Scottish Academic Press.

Meek, V. Lynn. 1992. "Quality and Relevance of Higher Education in Small States." Paper prepared for World Bank Small States Policy Seminar on Higher Education, Negara Brunei Darussalam, June 14–18. World Bank, Education and Social Policy Department, Washington, D.C.

Merrouni, Mekki. 1991. "L'Enseignement Supérieur au Maroc." World Bank, Education and Social Policy Department, Washington, D.C.

Mikhail, Sam. 1992. *The Non-University Sector of Higher Education in Developing Countries:A Survey of Recent Developments in Selected Countries*. Toronto, Canada: Ryerson International Development Centre.

Moock, Joyce L., and Peter R. Moock. 1979. *Higher Education and Rural Development in Africa: Toward a Balanced Approach for Donor Assistance*. New York: African-American Institute.

Muskin, Joshua A. 1992. "World Bank Lending for Science and Technology: General Operational Review." World Bank, Population and Human Resources Department, Education and Employment Division Background Paper Series PHREE/92/51R. Washington, D.C.

Mwiria, Kilemi. 1992. "University Governance: Problems and Prospects in Anglophone Africa." World Bank, Africa Technical Department, Education and Training Division, Technical Note 3. Washington, D.C.

Namuddu, Katherine. 1992. "Gender Perspective in African Higher Education." World Bank, Population and Human Resources Division, Technical Department, Africa Region. Washington, D.C.

Narsey, Wadan. 1992. "Brain Drain in Pacific Island States." Paper prepared for the World Bank Small States Policy Seminar on Higher Education, Negara Brunei Darussalam, June 14–18. World Bank, Education and Social Policy Department, Washington, D.C.

Nelson, Richard. 1986. "Institutions Supporting Technical Advance in Industry." *American Economic Review*, 76(2): 186–89.

———. 1990. "On Technological Capabilities and their Acquisition." In Robert Evenson and Gustav Ranis, eds., *Science and Technology: Lessons for Development Policy*. Boulder, Colo.: Westview.

Ngu, Jacob. 1992. "The Relevance of African Higher Education." World Bank, Population and Human Resources Division, Technical Department, Africa Region. Washington, D.C.

Ngu, Jacob L., K. Blackett Ngu, and J. C. Atangana. 1992. "Governance: The Cameroon Experience." World Bank, Education and Social Policy Department, Washington, D.C.

OECD (Organization for Economic Cooperation and Development). 1990. *Higher Education in California: Reviews of National Policies for Education*. Paris: OECD.

Oey-Gardiner, Mayling. 1992. "Higher Education in Indonesia: Past Performance and Future Challenges." World Bank, Education and Social Policy Department, Washington, D.C.

Olasiji, T. Dele, and Herbert R. Hengst. 1987. "Morale and Job Attitudes of Faculty and Administrators in a Nigerian University." Paper presented at the 31st Annual

Meeting of the Comparative and International Education Society. Arlington, Va.: Comparative and International Education Society.

Orivel, Francois. 1991. "French Speaking Universities in Sub-Saharan Africa, A Critical Impasse." *Propects* 21(3): 343–50.

Parker, Linda. 1992. "Industry-University Collaboration in Developed and Developing Countries." World Bank, Population and Human Resources Department, Education and Employment Division Background Paper Series PHREE/92/64. Washington, D.C.

Patel, I.G. 1991. "Higher Education and Economic Development: Keynote Address." Paper prepared for the World Bank Seminar on Innovation and Improvement of Higher Education in Developing Countries, Kuala Lumpur, Malaysia, June 30–July 4. World Bank, Education and Social Policy Department, Washington, D.C.

Paul, Jean-Jacques, and Laurence Wolff. 1992. "The Economics of Higher Education in Brazil." World Bank, Human Resources Division, Technical Department, Latin America and the Caribbean Region Paper 30. Washington, D.C.

Psacharopoulos, George. 1980. *Higher Education in Developing Countries: A Cost-Benefit Analysis* World Bank Staff Working Papers 440. Washington, D.C.: World Bank.

———. 1990. "Priorities in the Financing of Education." *International Journal of Educational Development* 10(2/3): 157–62.

———. 1991. "Higher Education in Developing Countries: The Scenario of the Future." *Higher Education* (Netherlands) 21(1): 3–9.

Ranis, Gustav. 1990. "Science and Technology Policy: Lessons from Japan and the East Asian NICs." In Robert Evenson and Gustav Ranis, eds., *Science and Technology: Lessons for Development Policy*. Boulder, Colo.: Westview.

Ransom, Angela. 1988. *Financing Higher Education in Francophone West Africa*. EDI Policy Seminar Report 12. Washington, D.C.: World Bank.

Regel, Omporn. 1992. "The Academic Credit System in Higher Education: Effectiveness and Relevance in Developing Countries". World Bank, Population and Human Resources Department, Education and Employment Division Background Paper Series PHREE/92/59. Washington, D.C.

Reiffers, J. L., and William Experton. 1992. "L'Enseignement Supérieur en Tunisie." World Bank, Education and Social Policy Department, Washington, D.C.

Research Institute for Higher Education. 1987. "Public and Private Sectors in Asian Higher Education Systems." Reports from Third International Seminar on Higher Education in Asia, Hiroshima University.

Richards, Alan. 1992a. "Higher Education in Central and Eastern Europe: Dilemmas and Opportunities of the Transition." World Bank, Education and Social Policy Department, Washington, D.C.

———. 1992b. "Higher Education in Egypt." Policy, Research, and External Affairs Working Paper WPS862. World Bank, Education and Social Policy Department, Washington, D.C.

Romain, Ralph. 1990. "Higher Education in Bank/IDA Lending." World Bank, Education and Social Policy Department, Washington, D.C.

Romer, Paul. 1990. "Endogenous Technical Change." *Journal of Political Economy*, 98 (5), Part 2, S71–102.

Rosenberg, Nathen. 1990. "Science and Technology Policy for the Asian NICS: Lessons from Economic History." In Robert Evenson and Gustav Ranis, eds., *Science and Technology: Lessons for Development Policy*. Boulder, Colo.: Westview.

Sack, Richard. 1991. "Higher Education in Algeria." World Bank, Education and Social Policy Department, Washington, D.C.

Saint, William. 1992. *Universities in Africa: Strategies for Stabilization and Revitalization*. World Bank Technical Paper 194. Washington, D.C.

Salmi, Jamil. 1984. "Educational Research on the Third World or with the Third World: A View from the South." *Institute of Development Studies Bulletin*, October 14(4). Brighton, U.K.

———. 1991a. "The Higher Education Crisis in Developing Countries." World Bank, Population and Human Resources Department, Education and Employment Division Background Paper Series PHREE/91/37. Washington, D.C.

———. 1991b. "Perspectives on the Financing of Higher Education." World Bank, Population and Human Resources Department, Education and Employment Division Background Paper Series PHREE/91/45. Washington, D.C.

Sawyer, Akilagpa. 1992. "Relations between Government and Universities in Ghana." World Bank, Education and Social Policy Department, Washington, D.C.

Schwartzman, Simon, and Lucia Klein. 1992. "Higher Education and Government in Brazil." World Bank, Education and Social Policy Department, Washington, D.C.

Scott, Maurice. 1989. *A New View of Economic Growth*. Oxford: Oxford University Press.

Selvaratnam, Viswanathan. 1991. "Meeting Human Resource Needs of Developing Countries: the Contribution of Overseas Education." Paper presented at the Conference on Overseas Education for Development, Princeton, New Jersey. World Bank, Education and Social Policy Department, Washington, D.C.

Selvaratnam, Viswanathan, and Omporn Regel. 1991. "Higher Education in the Republic of Yemen: The University of Sana'a." Policy, Research, and External Affairs Working Paper WPS676. World Bank, Education and Social Policy Department, Washington, D.C.

———. 1992. "Innovations in Higher Education: Singapore at the Competitive Edge." World Bank, Education and Social Policy Department, Washington, D.C.

Sesay, Allyson A. 1987. *Staff Productivity and Promotion in the Nigerian University System*. Sokoto: University of Sokoto.

Setapanich, Nongram, Supaporn Kohengkul, and Kuakul Chang-jai. 1992. "Higher Education in Thailand." World Bank, Education and Social Policy Department, Washington, D.C.

Sivalon, John. 1992. "The State and Higher Education in Tanzania." World Bank, Education and Social Policy Department, Washington, D.C.

Sutherland-Addy, Esi. 1992. "Access, Selection and Equity in African Higher Education." World Bank, Population and Human Resources Division, Technical Department, Africa Region. Washington, D.C.

Swamy, V. C. K. 1993. "The Open University." In P. G. Altbach and S. Chitnis, eds., *Higher Education Reform in India: Experience and Perspectives.* New Delhi: Sage Publications.

Tan, Edita A. 1991. "Mechanics of Allocating Public Funds to Universities: Their Implications on Efficiency and Equity." Paper prepared for the World Bank Seminar on Innovation and Improvement of Higher Education in Developing Countries, Kuala Lumpur, Malaysia, June 30–July 4. World Bank, Education and Social Policy Department, Washington, D.C.

Tan, Jee-Peng, and Alan Mingat. 1992. *Education in Asia: A Comparative Study of Cost and Financing.* Washington, D.C.: World Bank.

Teichler, Ulrich, Helmut Winkler, and Robert Kreitz. 1991. "Performance of Higher Education Measurements for Improvement: Evaluation of Outcomes." Paper prepared for the World Bank Seminar on Innovation and Improvement of Higher Education in Developing Countries, Kuala Lumpur, Malaysia, June 30–July 4. World Bank, Education and Social Policy Department, Washington, D.C.

Thulstrup, Erik W. 1992. "Improving the Quality of Research in Developing Country Universities." World Bank, Population and Human Resources Department, Education and Employment Division Background Paper Series PHREE/92/52. Washington, D.C.

Tindimubona, Alex R. 1992. "Research, Graduate Studies and Regional Cooperation in African Universities." World Bank, Population and Human Resources Division, Technical Department, Africa Region, Washington, D.C.

UNESCO. 1986. *The International Technological University.* Paris.

———. 1990. *L'Enseignement Supérieur au Benin: Bilan et Perspectives.* Cotonou: Mission Française de Coopération et d'Action Culturelle.

van Vught, Frans A. 1991. "Autonomy and Accountability in Government/University Relationships." Paper prepared for the World Bank Seminar on Innovation and Improvement of Higher Education in Developing Countries, Kuala Lumpur, Malaysia, June 30–July 4. World Bank, Education and Social Policy Department, Washington, D.C.

Weifang, Min. 1991. "A Comparative Study of Higher Education Development in Selected Asian Countries 1960–1990: Country Case Analysis of China." World Bank, Population and Human Resources Division, Technical Department, Asia Region, Washington, D.C.

———. 1992. "Autonomy and Accountability: An Analysis of the Changing Relationships Between the Government and Universities in China." World Bank, Education and Social Policy Department, Washington, D.C.

Williams, Gareth. 1986. "Internal Efficiency of Higher Education." World Bank, Population and Human Resources Division, Technical Department, Asia Region. Washington, D.C.

Winkler, Donald R. 1990. *Higher Education in Latin America: Issues of Efficiency and Equity.* World Bank Discussion Paper 77. Washington, D.C.

Woodhall, Maureen. 1992a. "Financial Diversification in African Higher Education." World Bank, Population and Human Resources Division, Technical Department, Asia Region, Washington, D.C.

————. 1992b. "Turning Points in the Development of Higher Education in Asia: A Comparative Study of Alternative Patterns of Provision, Finance and Governance, 1960–90." Paper for World Bank Senior Policy Seminar on Strengthening Public and Private Roles in Higher Education, Singapore, June 28–July 3. World Bank, Population and Human Resources Division, Technical Department, Asia Region, Washington, D.C.

World Bank. various years. *World Development Report*. New York: Oxford University Press.

————. 1978. "Review of Bank Operations in the Education Sector." World Bank, Operations Evaluation Department, Washington, D.C.

————. 1986a. *China: Management and Finance of Higher Education*. Washington, D.C.

————. 1986b. *Financing Education in Developing Countries: An Exploration of Policy Options*. Washington, D.C.

————. 1988. *Education in Sub-Saharan Africa: Policies for Adjustment, Revitalization, and Expansion*. A World Bank Policy Study. Washington, D.C.

————. 1990. *Primary Education*. A World Bank Policy Paper. Washington, D.C.

————. 1991a. "Indonesian Education and the World Bank: An Assessment of Two Decades of Lending." World Bank, Operations Evaluation Department Report 9752. Washington, D.C.

————. 1991b. *Vocational and Technical Education and Training*. A World Bank Policy Paper, Washington, D.C.

————. 1992a. "Access, Quality and Efficiency in Caribbean Education: A Regional Study." World Bank, Population and Human Resources Division, Country Department III, Latin America and the Caribbean Regional Office, Report 9753-CRG. Washington, D.C.

————. 1992b. "The Development of Scientific Research in the Maghreb." Education and Social Policy Department. World Bank, Education and Social Policy Department, Report 10515-MNA. Washington, D.C.

————. 1992c. "Pakistan: Higher Education and Scientific Research: Strategy for Development and Reform." World Bank, Education and Social Policy Department, Report 10884-PAK. Washington, D.C.

————. 1992d. "Revitalizing Higher Education in Senegal: The Challenge of Reform." World Bank, Population and Human Resources Division, Sahelian Department, Africa Region. Washington, D.C.

————. 1992e. "Strengthening the Policy Environment for Investment in University Development in Uganda." World Bank, Education and Social Policy Department, Washington, D.C.

————. 1992f. "World Bank Assistance to Agricultural Higher Education 1964–1990." World Bank, Operations Evaluation Department, Washington, D.C.

————. 1993. "The World Bank's Role in Human Resource Development in Sub-Saharan Africa." Washington D.C.

Wu, Kin Bing. 1992. "Higher Education in Hong Kong: Investment in Science and Technology During the Time of Political and Economic Change." World Bank, Population and Human Resources Department, Education and Employment Division Background Paper Series PHREE/92/70. Washington, D.C.

————. 1993a. "Science and Technology Education in Korea." World Bank, Education and Social Policy Department Discussion Paper Series. Washington, D.C.

————. 1993b. "Science and Technology Education in Taiwan [China]." World Bank, Education and Social Policy Department Discussion Paper Series. Washington, D.C.

Za'rour, George. 1988. "Universities in Arab Countries." Policy, Research and External Affairs Working Paper WPS62. World Bank, Education and Social Policy Department, Washington, D.C.

————. 1991. "Higher Education in Jordan." World Bank, Education and Social Policy Department, Washington, D.C.

Zhiri, Abdelwahed. 1991. "Higher Education in Selected Arab Countries: Issues of Efficiency and Employment." EDI Working Paper Series. World Bank, Economic Development Institute, Washington, D.C.

Ziderman, Adrian. 1990. "Universities and Development: The Evolving Role of the World Bank." World Bank, Education and Social Policy Department, Washington, D.C.